O.ARS 6/7:

VOICING

Editor:
 Don Wellman

Associate Editors:
 Cola Franzen
 Irene Turner

Contributing Editors:
 Robert Creeley
 Charles Bernstein
 Craig Watson

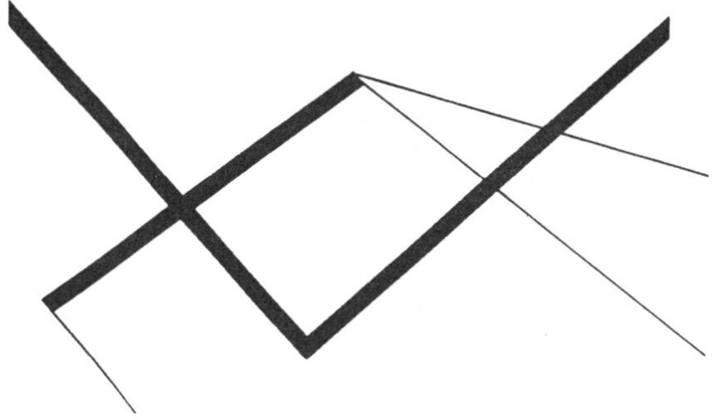

O.ARS

P.O. Box 814 // Cambridge MA 02139

Voicing has been published with the assistance of
The Massachusetts Council on the Arts and Humanities

New Series:

O.ARS will next appear in the January 1991. These are our current plans:

The new series will appear twice yearly, each issue varying in length from 60 to 90 pages. We will use desk-top publishing to get the news out and encourage timely response to new work or new directions. We will print reviews. Some issues may be devoted to the work of a single author or to a specific topic. *Authenticity, desire, liminality* are some topics that come to mind. Our interest will continue to be a poetic investigation of cosmos, polis, and self and we will continue to publish poetry, visual poetry, and experimental prose.

O.ARS is a revolving door and a windmill. The oar is a winnowing fan as well as a blade cutting the current. The thoughts or desires expressed in one number will continue, transformed or shifted along new axes of investigation: poem and statement evoking argument, manifesto, exegesis.

Your support is needed now. Producing *Voicing* has been a demanding experience. Hopefully this volume like our earlier endeavours, *Coherence, Perception, Translations*, will earn the respect of thoughful readers who truly value innovation and experiment. Your tax-deductible contribution ($50, $100 or more) will help us to meet current obligations and to build the financial base necessary for our future. Friends of O.ARS will receive a life-time subscription to the new series.

The subscription rate for the new series is $10.00 per year.

Special thanks to
Daniel Webster College
for its support in the production
of *Voicing*

O.ARS 6/7: *VOICING*
Copyright 1989, Don Wellman
ISBN 0 942030 08 7

O.ARS is distributed by:
Anton Mikofsky Distributing, 57 West 84th Street, #1C, New York, NY 10024
Segue Distribution, 303 East 8th Street, New York, NY 10012
Small Press Distribution, 1814 San Pablo Avenue, Berkeley CA 94702
Paul Green, 83b London Road, Peterborough, Cambs. U.K.

CONTENTS:

Preface:

The materials in this volume of O.ARS represent a variety of stances on voicing, a process that I understand as dialogic in nature and cumulative in its effects over time. For all of the physical ephemerality of the spoken word, voicing itself represents a continual sifting of the contents of memory. Voicing: speaking for oneself, speaking for others. Voicing is in a sense the founding act that constitutes the possibility of culture, community, or self. Voicing is a flow, whose beginning and end are equally indefinite or indeterminate, but whose course is subject to change, sometimes overflowing the banks, sometimes confined to channels, even as the rate of flow idles in meanders or plunges over rapids. Moreover, when any one of us voices our thoughts or feelings, *aye* or *nay* or even *maybe*, we weave and unweave, like so many Penelopes at our tapestry looms, the expanding and contracting matrix of desiring that holds us together. Voicing: the making and the measuring of home, polis, and cosmos.

Warning!

In compiling this collection, I have paid little attention to "voice" in its sense as the tone or quality that distinguishes one individual's soul stuff from another's. In "voicing" we are at one without violating the integrity of the many heterogeneous voices heard everywhere on all sides. Contrary to the constant propaganda broadcast over the airwaves (the US Pop/Commercial/Soap Opera culture), I do not believe that humanity is afflicted by a soullessness and has lost the ability to cry out. I am offended by the romantic image of the poetic self, an image of the poet as a special person possessing a deep feeling voice, more resonant than others. This ethos muffles the individual in vainglorious raptures, fostering a speaking without hearing, a mindless scattering of seed without loving the ground. Some have compared such writing to masturbation. I think it more a self-congratulatory frenzy, tossing beer cans, styrofoam cartons, and used condoms from the window of a lurching car like insecure juveniles. This paradigm is one of fear, fearing that others might discover who you are or what you do. My scenario requires many mouths and many ears, responsive, responding to one another, without hypocrisy.

--Don Wellman

IN MEMORIAM

Joel Oppenheimer
George Butterick

WAITING/ SEPT. '85

they are building
the dunes higher
bulldozing the beach
one hundred miles
south
          i huddle
behind glass and
wallboard
               waiting

its name is *gloria*
it moves north by
northeast chewing
the coast at twenty
miles per hour

in excelsis deo
says the song of
a different season

or *ad maiorem*
dei gloriam in
a different
society
          carrying
by sword

               oh a
pillar of cloud
by day

          they say
we should watch for tornadoes
which sometimes
accompany such
a storm on its
way inland

               the
first winter i
spent here we

worried about
earthquakes
               then
after three years
the worrying stopped
and a quake came

i wrote a poem
then too
               what else
should i do facing
the facts of life

so the pictures
of the dozers pushing
the beach up into
piles along the
ridge of dunes
and the mayor
speaking of what
precautions the
town had taken
stay in me to
sit with the mental
picture as a child
of knute ordering
the tide to fall back

yes i huddle
behind glass and
wallboard knowing
it will not

hoping god in his
greater glory and
the highest spares us this

winds as high as
a hundred sixty four
miles per hour
were registered at
blue hill in '38

that storm i walked
through the tail of
a kid just eight

head down clutching
at handholds on
the walls of buildings
i passed going home

and made it
*ad maiorem dei
gloriam* that day
survived to face
this one
                thinking
we are safe
snuggled in the
mountains

                we'll
see about that
say the winds
say the driving rain

as if sand or
glass made from
sand could protect
could fend off
you hurricano you

/John Viera

The Moon on 5th Avenue

SAYING AND SINGING

PL: Rhythm, humor, and play motivate the saying, are the sparks, the elements that unsettle the stories of Julio Cortázar as well as the songs of Saúl Yurkievich. Between the singer and the teller of tales there is an old complicity stimulated by this coincidence in the art of reviving discourse. For this reason I have brought you together, so that we can talk about prose and poetry, or rather about the avatars of the word in literature.

I consider that the two of you represent two literary genres, two different experiences in writing. To begin with you, Julio, you have made many multigeneric or intergeneric forays; you also write poetry sometimes. You insert poems into your prose and have compiled some of your poems in *Pameos y meopas*. What is your relationship with poetry, viewed from the central focus of your work which is the narrative?

JC: That question obliges me to go way back in my own life, even way back in history. I never forget that Greek philosophy did not begin with prose but with poetry. The pre-Socratics are poets and the first great philosophical text, by Parmenides, is a poem. And I would even go so far as to say that the work of Plato is that of a poet. The human race began expressing itself by means of poems. From a historical point of view, one would say that in the Greco-Latin world, poetry preceded prose, just as in man's infancy, poetry comes before prose. Verse has its own specific difficulties, but it allows completely free passage for feelings, intuitions, passions, something that does not happen in prose because of the requirement of communicability in prose. I began writing verses when I was between 8 and 12 years old, then after much difficulty I arrived at prose. What is true in the history of humanity is also true in the history of the individual. It seems to me that like every other human being I had an initial relationship with poetry; later I began to write stories or attempts at novels.

SY: Later you searched for another type of representation, other than the poetic.

JC: Yes, the world of pure sentiment, that of elegy, love, nostalgia, that I experienced through poetry, I tried to relocate in a terrain proper for ideas, action and description that belongs to prose. But I never abandoned poetry. The first two books I published were of poetry: a collection of sonnets and *Los Reyes (The Kings)* that I have always considered a poem in prose. Nobody knows exactly what a prose poem is, but to me the language of *The Kings* is poetic.

SY: *The Kings* is a dramatic poem.

JC: Right. It has a setting of scene, and also a discussion of genres, and there I don't accept either the classification of verse or of prose for it. The text is written in prose but with poetical intention. The internal rhythm shows that I am more focused on the poetic than on the prosaic.

I have written poems all my life. Some have been collected in *Pameos y meopas*, a slightly ironic and affectionate title using two anagrams of *poemas*. My feeling of embarrassment about my poetry comes from the fact that none of my friends like my poems but are immediately very enthusiastic about my prose. My friends, as well as the Argentinian critics, classify me as a prose writer. This caused me to consider poetry as a private activity. Only in recent years, my fear of public reaction lost, did I start to insert poems of mine into some of my books, particularly in my almanacs.

SY: You make a distinction between prose and poetry that should be clarified. I believe it would be more accurate if we distinguish between narrative and poetry. The specifics of the narrative genre would not be the gnomic, because poetry is not free of meaningful message; the specific would be the anecdotal, the anecdotal as a recountable experience like a fable. In your case, do you have a special predilection, feel a particular delight or joy in the anecdotal?

JC: Yes, I do. Ever since my childhood I have been attracted by what you call the anecdotal, that is, by specific situations that require narration with a before and an after, with a coherence that develops within a certain time, even though the time may be fantastic.

SY: Attracted by the story, by the story first rather than by the discourse.

JC: By the story of the imaginary that rarely coincides with the so-called real. You know very well, Saúl, that most of my stories are of a fantastic type, but that doesn't make them any less real for me.

PL: And you, Saúl, what motivates your texts?

SY: I myself am motivated by visions. I never have narrative glimpses. My visions strike suddenly, or rather they are visions of states. I never see reality as a narrative plot, as an illation. I see the world as a hodge-podge, a steam-rolling conglomeration of things, like an incomprehensible multiplicity. For this reason I believe that history is an artificial construction, I consider it more a result of reading than of actual, factual events. I can never see stories because everything gets jumbled together in a muddle, all mixed up. My vision is not fixed, it doesn't write stories, it doesn't come structured as a story. I never think in terms of stories.

JC: You have never written anything that might be called a story?

SY: I have written mythical stories. I tell them as though they were dreams. They appeal to me as a means of distancing, through their symbolic suggestion. They do not seek the cohesion of action; they lack psychological depth. They are purely factual, lineal. There is no plot.

JC: For me, a story is just the opposite.

SY: No doubt. You are a master of the plot-within-a-plot narrative.

JC: Our points of departure are different. For me, a story worthy of the name presupposes the development of a mechanism, a machine consisting of a given set of elements, either previous or final, that arranges and defines itself and so acquires its autonomy as a story. It is completely separate from any other genre: it is not a fragment of a novel, it is not a poem in prose, it is not the recounting of a dream. It is not fragmentary.

SY: I see only the fragmentary. I can plan the functioning of the poetic machine so that it will work efficiently, but not its total organization. I cannot conceive of a closed form, that would take on a sharp outline, be completely delineated.

JC: When you speak of the closed quality of forms you are describing the *sine qua non* of the short story, but not the novel. I tend to conceive of the novel as an open work.

SY: As for me, if I close a work it is for a rhetorical or parodic effect, because I am playing with stereotypes, with conventions. In your writing, Julio, there is a greater semantic determination on all levels than in mine; there is a powerful personal presence, a passion, a will to convey a message.

JC: But we agree with each other, because that vision of the fragmentary that strikes you, I apply to the novel. It seems to me that *Rayuela (Hopscotch)* is a book that is dizzyingly open, full of holes and openings. It is absolutely the opposite of my stories.

SY: In *Hopscotch* you use, as I do in my *Fricciones (Frictions)* a system of *collage* that allows one to assemble a heterogenous multiplicity of components that do not lose their essential quality. They are woven together but not reduced to a common denominator. A dialectic vision, contrasting, unresolved, not circumscribed by a determination to harmonize that would string them together, that would integrate everything into a representation that is, if not univoiced, at the very least is unifying. The same thing occurs with your almanacs, *La vuelta al dia en ochenta mundos (Around the Day in Eighty Worlds)* and *Ultimo round (Last Round)*.

JC: Well, you have to be careful with the almanacs. Actually these books were not intended as a work, they don't have the intention of unity proper of a work. They are an accumulation of independent texts. To some extent they are born of nostalgia for those almanacs of my childhood that the country people used to read and that contained a little bit of everything, from home remedies and puericulture to ways of planting carrots, and even poems. The only unity possible in my almanacs lies in the writing, it comes from the fact that all of the texts were written by me. I like these books especially because they go against the notion of genre, a notion very much in disarray now but one that still creates havoc. Still today critics and readers feel uncomfortable when they can't classify a work.

SY: The interpenetration, transfusion, the circle of interconnecting vessels that has managed, if not to abolish, at least to blur, the fixed lines between genres in the Latin American novel, began above all as a result of your work. You are the one who started it.

JC: So say the critics, and also, even a poet like you.

SY: Historically speaking, I don't recall an earlier precedent; if it's a question of chronology, I don't see another more decisive antecedent. I also believed and believe in the interpenetration of genres, but the turn of Latin American poetry toward the prosaic and the anecdotal now appears to me to have a negative effect. Obviously the poetry of the 1950s was too solemn, too sublime, too far removed from the local and the actual, too ahistorical, too remote from our immediate experience. Then there came a push to connect poetry with the world of ordinary people, with everyday life, with concrete reality, by bringing it down to a level where it could record in the spoken language, the living language, the restrictions of the empirical real. Our poetry turned conversational (it is also described as prosaic or colloquial poetry) domestic, popular, man-in-the-street language. But there was such an irruption of the immediate, the raw, the unshaped, the untransformed, that the excessive prosiness ended by seeming insignificant to me. It bores me.

JC: Don't you think, Saúl, that the opposite phenomenon has also occurred in prose, that there was an irritating amount of the poetic in prose? What Alejo

Carpentier insisted on calling baroque, considering it a distinctive sign of Latin American literature, but what else is it except an avalanche of poetical vocabulary, of metaphors, of alliterations, metonymies, that overload the prose and turn every description into a kind of great bejewelled pectoral? The baroque bores me, except in its most amusing forms, except in Lezama Lima.

SY: Then the specificity of each genre will have to be reinforced: poetry must be made more poetical and prose more prosy.

JC: The proper rhythm for each separate expression must be found. When I published my first stories, those of *Bestiario*, the first that were publishable, I noticed in the reading of them something I had felt while writing them. It was what we might call a beat; we can call it rhythm, if we are careful not to mix it up with the *soi disant* poetical rhythm similar to that found in the prose of a Gabriel Miró. No, it is absolutely not that; it is a matter of a kind of pulsation that is most emphatically not based on poetical rhythms, hendecasyllables or alexandrines; it has nothing to do with the number of syllables, although there could possibly be a connection since we are dealing with words. There is no deliberate search for a rhythmic measure. When I write I feel the rhythm of what I am telling, but that comes from inside a pulsation. When I feel that this rhythm stops and the sentences enter a terrain that we might call prosaic, I realize I have taken a wrong turn and I stop. I know that I have failed. This is noticeable above all at the end of my stories, the end is always a long sentence, or an accumulation of long sentences that have a perceptible rhythm when read aloud. I always require my translators to watch that rhythm, to find the equivalent because without it, even if the ideas and the sense are there, the story would fall apart.

PL: It is as though in the end, in the final sentences, you have the sensation of discovering the rhythm that you were searching for all along, throughout all the other pages. Where does this feeling come from, of something satisfactorily ended?

JC: From a feeling of fate. Those sentences are born from that rhythm. They are not ideas based on the rhythm. It is as though the rhythm and whatever is being said are the same. They are totally fused, and that is what gives them the character of a fated thing.

PL: In other words such a rhythm arises more from the grammatical structure than from syllabic rhythm. And what about syllabic rhythm, do you find it crude?

JC: No, I don't find it crude or less interesting. I think that the syllabic is included also in this other rhythm. I remember particularly the end of the title story of *Bestiario*, where it would not have been possible to substitute any adjective of four syllables for one of three, even though it might have been more accurate as to sense; but it would lose its accuracy of sense if it didn't fit into the rhythm. Everything had to be within that rhythmic mold and I believe it is the mold that gives sense to the sentence.

SY: That is the perfect definition of poetic period, when the selection of words is not made by free substitution but is mandated by contiguity; the imposing element comes from the sonorous surroundings.

PL: In prose written in Spanish, which writers do you find most satisfying, from the point of view of rhythm?

JC: Lezama Lima is one of the most satisfactory, despite his many clumsy constructions that I don't feel are important compared to his many successes. The rhythmic period of Lezama Lima coincides exactly with what he is feeling and putting into words. I like certain chapters of *El Señor Presidente* of Asturias and above all *Hombres de Maíz (Men of Maize)* where there is a chapter called "Venado de las siete rosas" ("Stag of the Seven Roses") that is of a marvelous rhythmic perfection. Some moments of Alejo Carpentier.

PL: I wasn't thinking of modern authors when I asked the question. What about the classics?

JC: Don Quixote. The rhythm of Cervantes is incredible. Not always, obviously, because what I call pulsation or rhythm should have, as in music, moments of climax, moments of extreme tension, that cannot be sustained, otherwise they would end up being monotonous. And there must be moments of distension that are more prosaic in order to permit the explosion of the culminating passages to acquire maximum force. The great discourses of Quixote are of such rhythmic beauty that they seem miraculous to me. Another of my great loves is *La Celestina.* The rhythm of the last fifteen pages of *La Celestina* is unequalled in all the rest of Spanish literature put together.

PL: And you, Saúl, what do you think of rhythm?

SY: I agree essentially with Julio. For me the basic rhythm is alliterative, it is established by phonation through a sonorous relationship that is produced by one's own imposition of saying, by the internal dynamic of the word. It is a pulsational rhythm. There is no other satisfactory definition. Every attempt of rhythmic analysis ends by being insufficent because the rhythm returns the language to the articulatory base of the phonic, returns it to the bodily depths. It is kinetic, it is a natural force, profound, a return to a semanticism that is primitive, original, organic. For me the homophony is more of a determining factor than the homology, the phonetic relationship more important than the conceptual. I believe in the chance finds provoked by the rhythmic pulsation that arouses its own associations, conjunctions or constellations of sense.

JC: The rhythm discovers the sense, the rhythm is an awakener of senses.

SY: The rhythm is a liberator of sense, a very effective liberator because every liberation has to have a limit so as not to fall into total disorder. Rhythm provides a boundary and invites such semantic amplitude that it appears everything can enter. Vibrant, it is a pulsating entity that imposes its own vectors.

PL: You speak of alliterative rhythm but you write in verse. Alliteration is also found in prose. I suppose that verse poses problems for you that Julio doesn't have.

SY: That's right. I have to resolve the problem of the line break, specific to poetry. Verse demands a pre-determined type of formalization, a periodization that also exercises a rhythmic function. Verse is the shaper by antonomasia of poetic discourse. Having accepted this determination, my problem is to rid myself of the traditional versification of the Spanish language. This versification is so rooted in our rhythmic perception, so interrelated with the sonorous economy of our language that it is very difficult to escape from it. If I let myself go with complete spontaneity, I am a poet of hendecasyllables, an eleven-syllable poet. It is such a paradox: my spontaneity is a regulated spontaneity because it is a conditioned spontaneity.

JC: Don't forget that the hendecasyllable is the natural breath of the Spanish language and when I am writing prose, hendecasyllables come out constantly.

SY: No doubt. I have not made a rhythmic analysis of your prose, but if I did, it is very likely that I would find in it a hendecasyllabic economy.

PL: You, Saúl, fight against the hendecasyllable...

SY: ...the hendeca, the hendecasy...

PL: ...the hendecasasyllabilism

SY: ...the hemmedenacaboosyllabism.

PL: So you fight against this pattern while Julio accepts it, submerging it in the verbal flow.

JC: I accept it because when I am writing I am not aware that I am writing hendecasyllables.

PL: Saúl, you suffer from an awareness of a traditional form, while Julio moves around at his ease in an unconscious acceptance of it. Who has helped you to counter the hendecasyllable in your poetry?

SY: In our own contemporary poetry I don't find much help in countering the influence of the hendecasyllable. Neruda has helped me a great deal, the Neruda of *Residencia en la Tierra (Residence on Earth)*.

JC: Huidobro, also.

SY: Huidobro, through his work of deconstructing. In Huidobro there is a search that is rhetorical, formalistic; there is a dismantling of the hendecasyllable and an experimentation of great technical breadth. In Huidobro the notion of technique is very much in evidence. Neruda is the opposite, his oracular, psalmodic discourse seems like a natural flow alien to all geometry, to all playful manipulation.

PL: We have talked at length about rhythm, let's go on now to the attitude that each of you has toward play.

SY: Play for me is absolutely essential as a way to remove pathos and to demythify. Play always implies distance, doubling, duplicity. It serves to counter the totalitarian intentions of the instinct, the sentimental take-over. It constitutes an ever-ready weapon against every type of oppression. Play empties out the pigeonholes, jolts one out of customary conditioning. To play implies to un-automate, to un-codify. To play with chance means to open oneself to the unusual, to work with surprising virtualities, with prodigious potentials. From the formal point of view, play is the most prodigal attitude because it establishes a relationship of limited responsibility with the object; it permits one to deal with it without an excess of loyalty, without total identification, it permits one to take it apart irreverently, to turn it topsy-turvy. Play is the agent by antonomasia of transformations.

PL: How can play be introduced into poetry?

SY: It is introduced in various ways: by working with chance relationships, by working gratuitously, working on the surface. Play breaks with normal continuity, the usual. Since it is ruled by the pleasure principle, it is a rupture of utilitarian realism. It transports us to a zone of exception, where we recover free will. It can be used when there is no desire to impart a serious bit of knowledge, when there is no desire to convert the discourse into a vehicle to express a profound experience. In this sense play for me is a de-psychologizer. It de-egoizes.

PL: Do you introduce chance into your poetry?

SY: Yes, by practicing a completely free kind of writing that is not automatic writing, because it never implies going into a state of trance.

JC: You mean a game of free association of words, one dragging the other by the tail.

SY: Exactly. It is also a matter of irreverence, playful irreverence, the opposite of being carried away. I do not believe in the poetic efficacy of hallucinatory states.

JC: Well, I would say that more than not believing in them, they don't exist in you. They can exist in others.

SY: Yes, Julio, in you.

PL: Aside from chance, are there other uses of play in your poetry?

SY: Yes, another consists of using all the combining possibilities of the language. There are very regulated games such as those built around the variations of a formal canon. One can carry symmetry to the extreme, or provoke disorder, dispersion. I can collect stereotypes, ready-made expressions, and activate them by means of unusual mixtures. I can use rhyme and carry it to an extreme, think up a poem where there is not only final rhyming but the maximum of internal rhyming.

PL: And you, Julio, do you agree with Saúl's conception of play?

JC: I agree completely with his theory of play, with that topology and typology of the playful, with the delimitations he has set forth. Now, as for me, because we are now talking about my relationship with the playful, a game is a very serious idea. Ever since I was a child, and now more than ever, every game that is a real game, that is not a farce or a momentary diversion, that is, games as children play them, and as I as a writer try to play them, correspond to archetypes, they come from very deep, from the collective unconscious, from the memory of the species. I believe that the game is a desacralized form of all that sacred ceremonies connoted for humanity. When I was writing *Hopscotch* I thought about giving it a more pretentious title. I thought about calling my book *Mandala*. Then it seemed pedantic to me and I remembered that hopscotch is a mandala, except that children play it without any idea of sacredness; then I adopted the hopscotch as a symbol of a tentative metaphysics, as a mystical search that presupposes an initiation and a trial, because one has to advance with the stone from square to square and there's always the possibility of failure, of never reaching Heaven. There is the usual hopscotch, the one that French children play and there is the spiral, snailshell hopscotch that we also played in Argentina. The spiral is the Cretan labyrinth; the labyrinth, one of the first archetypical symbols of humanity, it is a sign of mystery, of going toward the unknown to discover a central secret. I believe that the game is a survival in us of a contact with very deep forces that we now see less clearly.

PL: In the Cardplayers of Cezanne, the two so hieratic figures seem to be carrying out a ritual act.

JC: When I was a young fellow I played a lot of poker which is a very serious game; we didn't play for large sums of money, because to do that one has to have some money. We played for pleasure. By confronting various adversaries in poker one can define oneself, find the key and the answer to such important things as friendship or love. I have experienced this myself; I discovered the secret of a friend in a game of poker. In a game many more things come to light that go much farther than just winning or losing.

PL: How do you reflect this playful attitude in your literature? For example, how is it shown in *Hopscotch*?

JC: The playful elements are very numerous in *Hopscotch*. The structure of the novel itself is an invitation to play a game. I propose two readings, but many others are possible. This idea of game, I have explained, expressed in a much more conscious manner in *62 Modelo para armar (62 A Model Kit)*. There the subtitle provides the reader with an opening so that he can play his own game. The notion of a game appears in many of my stories, above all in "Final de Juego" ("End of the Game") that announces the idea in the title. "Manuscrito hallado en un bolsillo" ("Manuscript Found in a Pocket"), from *Octohedron*, is a game of life or death played in the Paris Metro. It concerns a man who imposes the rules of a game on himself in the search for a woman, and he will win or lose depending on whether the woman chooses a certain connection or not. He is compelled to comply with the rule and he loses. The title indicates that he throws himself between the wheels of a subway train. I believe that in this story I have shown the maximum fidelity that I am capable of to the playful. It is a game to the death such as the ones the gladiators played, and don't forget that in *Todos los fuegos el fuego (All Fires the Fire)* there is a combat between gladiators.

PL: Do you know anyone who has applied this conception of game to his own life?

JC: Not personally, but I suppose that someone like Marcel Duchamp places himself in a playful position toward life; life for him is an immense vertiginous game. Another example would be R. Roussel.

SY: Speaking of Duchamp, in his last exhibition in Paris two works were shown that were done in Buenos Aires. The one that might interest you most, Julio, is a pencil drawing over a photograph of the Rio de la Plata; over that sepia-colored monotony Duchamp drew an octahedron in the form of a double pyramid.

JC: Really, I didn't know that. But on the other hand, maybe you will remember that in *Last Round* I cite Duchamp's game with packing twine during his stay in Buenos Aires. In *Hopscotch* I imagined a similar scene without knowing that Duchamp had ever been in Buenos Aires. These happenings prove to me that chance plays its cards very well. Chance is a word I don't believe in.

PL: What is the role of humor in your work?

JC: From very early times, since I began to write, humor has been tied to what I wrote. A large part of Spanish literature seems tedious and heavy to me because it is completely lacking in humor. From the time I was very young I was an enthusiast of Anglo Saxon literature. The sense of humor is an invention and a property of the English. No literature has greater humorists than the English. What attracted me most was the discovery that the English, including Shakespeare, often used humor to say profoundly dramatic and even tragic things, thus relieving them of bad taste, tackiness, and the overblown quality they have when they lack humor. The English use humor for extremely serious ends. It is enough to see how and when it appears in the literature, it appears in culminating moments to remove the truculent or the tragic. This seems to me a great lesson, not only a literary lesson but a lesson for life. I have always tried to live my life using my sense of humor to establish a certain distance before certain situations and to be able to see them with more depth than would be possible without that distance. This humor came out in many of my texts, above all in my novels. For example, there are situations in *Hopscotch* that would be unbearable if they did not have some humor in them, a sense of humor very serious at times. The scenes that are most terrible, most dramatic need humor to get by, to be acceptable. And in *Libro de Manuel (Manual for Manuel)* the humor is absolutely necessary to provoke the upset of the Great Conventions of society to make way for a more humane order. The sense of humor is a constant in my novels, because the short story, as a genre, doesn't mix very well with humor...

SY: And *Historias de Cronopios y Famas (Stories of Cronopios and Famas)?*

JC: I don't consider them stories. For me a story has a plot, it consists of a closed sphere within which a dramatic action is developed.

SY: Then *Stories of Cronopios and Famas* are sketches.

JC: Call them whatever you please, call them sketches, or vignettes, as the Cubans say.

PL: And for you, Saúl, what is humor?

SY: Humor is the art of reversal, the antidote to all excess of determinism, to all fatalism. Humor is the greatest contravener of solemnity. It is a vaccine against all despotic hegemony. It is the great desacralizer. Like the game, it consists of a technique of substraction, of distension, of distancing. Against the pathetic avalanche, against frenetic inflation, against vital urgency, it produces a playful cut, an ironic splitting apart, a liberating aside. I think of the many kinds of humor: surprising humor that disarranges writing, that wrecks the expected; black humor that sets aside moral norms and the affective imperative; I think of that game of echoes, in those speculative bifurcations that parodic humor or ironic humor produce, or the reductions to the absurd that nonsensical humor brings about. I think above all of verbal humor, the best dis-automating device of the language, the most efficacious diversifier, disarranger. Because only humor can bring out the most bizarre mixtures, the most heterogenous marriages. Humor is the art of the surface, it refloats what is heavy and sinks what is light. Humor clips my wings but it pulls me out of a black hole.

PL: That is, according to Saúl, humor is a defense mechanism against oneself and against the world. It is a distance...

JC: It is a distance, yes, but it is a distance that comes close. If it is not an escape mechanism, it is a distance that allows us to see better. We Latin Americans need humor especially.

PL: Why Latin Americans in particular?

SY: Because in Latin America there is a tendency toward solemnity that stiffens and takes away ductility.

PL: I see. If one keeps in mind the horrible situation of Latin America, perhaps the only way to think of it with a certain freedom might be by means of humor.

JC: That's what I wrote in the brief prologue of *Manual for Manuel* that caused such indignation among the militant comrades; they believe that humor has nothing to do with the revolution. I believe that it does have something to do with it. In Latin America, I wage two great battles, one for the liberation of humor and the other for the liberation of the erotic, for a humourousness and an eroticism that are whole and that will free us from all the taboos that come to us, above all, from the Hispanic tradition. I fight against the "tortugones amoratados", or the bruised humongous turtles, as Lezama Lima would say.

SY: In Latin America we are waging battles against all oppressors, against the censors and against the commissars.

JC: Against the commissars who have no sense of humor and on top of that are lousy lovers.

Speech Pattern Playback Device

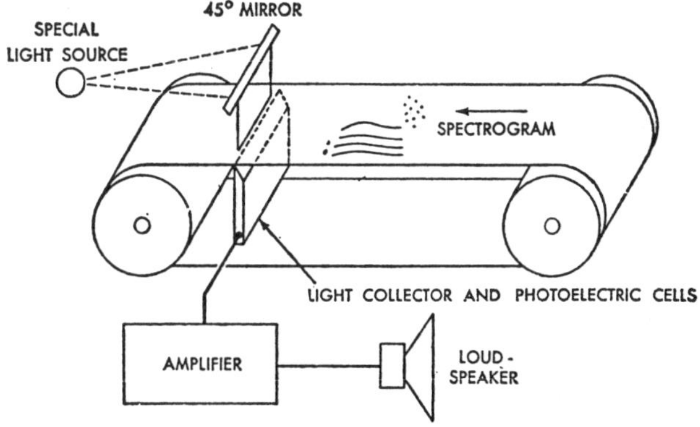

Voice-prints:

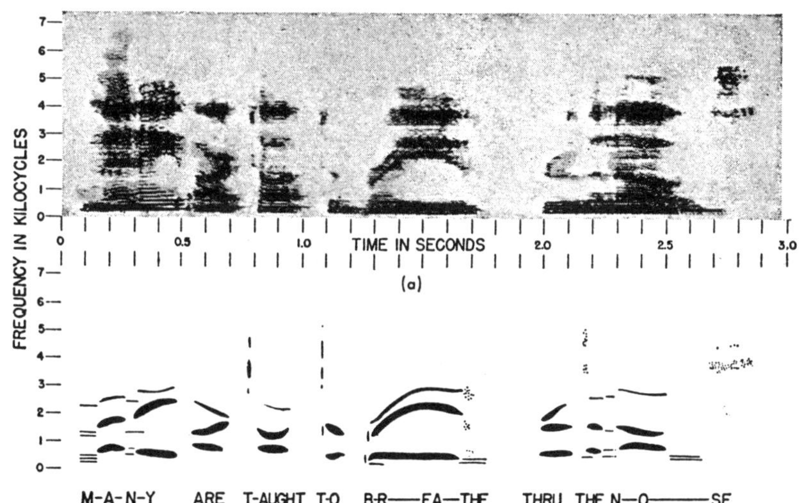

Voicing 14

BACKGROUND NOISE

```
tenebrous      turbid      turmoil      turbulence
                                          background noise
swarming storms
of senseless boomings
no voice        rasps        astounds            founders
    outcry            shrieks          clamor            howls
        shadow of beclouded              clusters
   storm clouds    without contours              without confines
            mass that densifies
fusing fervor                    seesaw
            mass that rarefies
                            mish-mash of meteors
                            scoriae side by side
booms        bundles bundle up        bubbling
   discharges                detaches          dissolves
            torrid                metrorrhagia
                            in the commotion
retreats        rations            remarks
        replicas        repeat
            as long as    as long as
        tempo            syncope
                    rate    aim    mark    mold
                    cusp    borne    myth    bound
tenuous synchrony
                against the great uproar
                against the thundersquall
orbital time
        eclipses      ellipses      orbs
                            measure off
the clockmakers
                regulate their just so and their exactly
pendulum world
                pole                crystal            planet
rare      crest            still            oasis            of quiet
                                        in the disquiet
suspension points            spores
                                    in the morass
stops                        jots
                                    in the upheaval
                                    in the whole errancy
            disorder precedes order
            and only that is real
```

great number   cloud number
            the innumerable precedes limitation
            and only that is real
at the threshold
            hodgepodge   farrago   background fracas
                                raucus ruckus
(shake well before using)   bedlam
      lawless   nameless   shapeless
         leaderless   tumult
                         vociferous tumult

in the beginning is the tempest
                              rupture

viral dissemination
                black box   opacity
                               of dispersion
undifferentiated   aggregate   join
          profuse   myriads   conglomerating
                                       squandering
infinite probability of disorder
                              vertigo
against the raving   in face of frenzy
            the capsule   the cubicle
domain of the eyedropper   pharmacopoeia of the pill
      extract   quadrant
the clockmakers rule
            fitters   machinists   manufacturers
      accountants
            assess   adjust   mark   square and cube
      measurers
            make commensurate   make chronometric
gnomon   chronomy   nodes
      nomenclators
            pigeonhole   catalog   subordinate
      geometers arrange boxes
            enclose orbicular orbs
            in contraptions of crystalline spheres
            regulate
                 the centers   the axes   the chords
eye and sun   analogs   particle and planet
            score the celestial music
            parallel the orders
            project concordant perspectives
         stereographers   axonometrics
the mandatories   the preceptors   the pardoners
            dictate   sanction   legislate
                 the legitimate

                                        the confirmation
          theatre of shadows   fable   chimera
          figurations   omni opera   trickery
          to conjure up a universe against the clangor of the crucible
a universe   no
a multiverse   upside down
                                        inside out
          without pole
          without repose
                              indifferent to the cosmographer's dream
                              to the pull of gravitation
                                                            outlet
burning furnace
             in hazardous agitation
not clock but conflagration
not cadence but candescence
                         fire
                         every body   possesses it
                         receives it   contains it
                         conducts it   and passes it on
racket   gurgle   bustle
     clamor   without number
                              without name
disorder precedes order
and only that is real
                         cloud
                         whole without exterior
transverberation
               migrant heat
        transfers   transits
cumulus
        rise   fall   run
          tremor   eruption   shifting
        there is no staying
        there is no constancy
        there is no consistency
                              only circumstance
                              that is alternation
                                            come what may
translations   transfusions   transsubstantiations
everything is altered   becomes alien
              everything   is consumed
jabber   jumbled worm-nest
                                    boiling
clouds of eletrons   gyrating clusters
              roseate rosiness
                  reckless rapture
hornet's nest   exorbitant   gnawing

                                        termite tunnels
                convulsive outcry
                          spurts out in a gush
                intensities   against   resistances
powerful fields
                passages   clogs   knots
     inch by inch   the difference   motor mix-up
                plenary agitation
                  and all in all withal above all
                  and all in all of all the all
                          in all and for all
                          all for all
inflamed air
          the states veer vacillate
                                that one
          that one that changes its name
                but that has no name
        contraction   condensation   dilation
smoke   fog   blast   dust
all ablaze   all candescent   but extinguishable
                whether to be dissected
                whether to be dispersed
                whether to be undone
ruddy aurora   burning morning
                of the conflagration
vortex before the outline and the listing
          jumbled clappers   clanging   onslaught
                                                        babel
                                  fundamental rigamarole
          free-for-all   farrago
morning turbulence of constitutions
                                corpuscular bodies
momentaneous separations
shifting differences
                        hoarse   regurgitation
                        from the resounding
                                        underground
mother tongue
            raw material
      matrix
            of the ventriloquial properties
          plethora   pile-up   profusion
          by the barrel   in bulk
                                bulkily
in the tangle of beginnings   of assaults
                of the first stockpile
                of the radical accumulation
                                        before

Voicing 18

before the differentiation
        the explosion
        the partitura
        the fine cutting
        the minutia
before might happen
                        the faint-heartedness of the alveoles
                        whatever prevents hearing the bald cry
                        the living voice suddenly
                                call from the depths
                                the chattering from below
                                                inside
before the catalog
                in the time of formlessness
crisscross of monsters
                senseless assemblies
        anybody at all   anywhere at all
                        contradiction
        before the ordinal   before the numeral
confused primer   helter
                                        skelter
                        unseeable   unsayable
the nature of the real in the air
the inconstant power
vastness of the opening   in the open
before substraction
before sheepfolds
        the reserve of the reticulum
        illusion of the enclosing cloud
        of the circle that fixes fluxes
        of the obedient system
        of the balance of forces
                                mechanical world
        organ/appartus/artifact
                        captive force
                        isolated holding
                        of the nebular furnace
        meshings   synchronies: ingenuous arts
before Pandora's box was opened
wreck that wipes out inscription
        that annuls every prescription
                                expansive excess
            razes account and reason
                                restores midday
the solar arrogance
                the one that speaks not
                the one that writes not
                                unmodeled

                                        immoderate
burning cloud
                force of maximum unpredictability
                force of the highest improbability
brute force
                without precession without succession
                without condition without germ
                not first motor: antimotor
farther or nearer the cyclical sky
in the first or the last instance
                but it is not point
                        is not center
                        is not head
        not a circumstance with limit
        a circumstance without limit
        spark of the burning
lightning stroke   neither cipher nor flourish nor blemish
    doesn't style doesn't note doesn't brand
                                only consigns congealed
        streak of carbon
                                to the bark of the split tree
cry from the red gullet   mouthed
                        to become word
                        crystallized in icy cackle
        word of the glassy eyes
                beak piercing   bone-dry
        word without light
                        niggard nightfall
                        nattering
        marrow parched
        barren land baked clay
        islets of settlement
                consent
                        in the middle
of the turbid thundering jumble
            sounds sound amid the uproad
living language deafened by nonsense clamorings
        cadence/singsong/mumblemumble
                                against the capricious chorus
        manna   rosemead   against pandemonium
thunder   lightning
                        fiery advent
        power to hold   against power of dispersion
flaming arrow
                potency imprisoned
                by ensnaring bonds
freed
        cuts through disorder

consummate word   consumed   disappears
fixed word   founders
word loosened by chance collisions
                        dissipates and falls
                                goes
            haywire
perhaps
     not every event will find its witness
     history   elllipsis   machine
                                a bare
          bit of boldness
     spark   point   drop   crack
     tablet   tessera   annal   stela
          scanty slogans   redraft
     the letter is contemptuous of catastrophe
     pen saved from the stormy surf
     bottle from the whirlpool
     counterweight   countermark   counterseal
     countermanding the dispersion
     edge   blade   thin thread
        spins   fancies
                        about its treasure island:
     storehouse of alphabets past and future
     every gloss   every glyph
     the complete glyphary   testaments
(time corroded the chronicles but could not erase one letter of the
history that the ibis carries engraved on the shell of its egg)
the comet marks the night
                    ethereal note resplendent flourish
                    rim rimming the whirlwind
                                signals
                    the death of the immortals
                    end of the empirical
                    Pan and Apollo succumb
the tempest increases
noise of the lawless underground
                    stormclouds thunder
                    the hurricane carries away
                                the orbs
                    disperses them
                                buries them
                    in a dustcloud
star dust
        disasters of stars
    the world is a rare edge
              tellable   singable
              between two whirlwinds
                        crest

                    between precipices
                                    balanced ball
                                    spinning
pencil point
brittle
                in the beginning of the word is the disaster
                coming before   and   coming after
isthmus between
two oceans   logos
                      lightning flash in the wild night
                      seized between feverish storms
slantwise past
the upheaval   silences   sets down his supply of words
                           his Rosaceae
                           knife-edge suspended between earth and noise
                trick   geometrical truce
                    there happens between wars
                after the uproar
                    the hand-to-hand combat
                    there comes after
                                    the war cry
                                    the murderous blows
                                    the drawing and quartering
                                    the clash of arms
                                                and the havoc
                                    of gigantomachy
            fusing language   ballooning brouhaha
from the handful   to mountainous heaps   scattering
                jumble   serpentarium
                    nest of worms
riot   rout
                              not peroration
                              plethora
                                        vociferant
barbarous language
                  chestnuts exploding in the coals
                  streak that slits the tempestuous tenebrosity
                  clamor in the tumult of the cyclones
                                    disorder precedes order
                                    and only that

VOICE // VOICING // VOICES

A FORUM ON THE THEME OF VOICING:

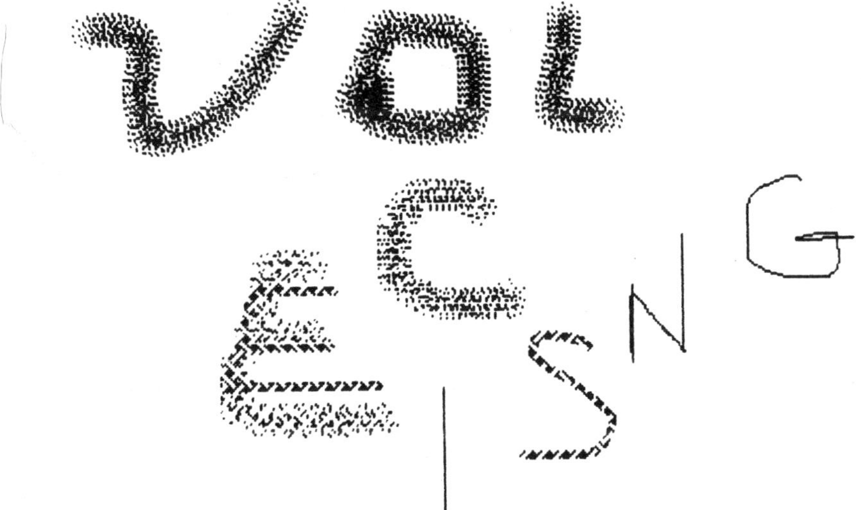

these ornaments tell the musician how to
shape the voice line

in voicing the choice of colors is made

the voices in their colors sing

voice//voicing//voices
Each voice is itself
Each voicing contains
          transmits its voices

I//am   sending//we can be heard   exist

/Charles Morrow

VOX: EX NIHILO?

Voice: out of what or where? We know little, nothing about how thoughts come to mind, voice comes to throat. Probably together, inseparable. From inside, or outside? In the latter case, dictated from out there, from above? In the former: usually from a great depth. Above and below as opposites in the world model? Or both: out of the not-*here*, the there, the elsewhere?

In *Popol Vuh*, Maya voice, voices, co-emerge with world, are world (vibrations) at the beginning. Depth analogy: voice sources out of *silence*. Most dialectics offer that: voice/silence; silence/voice. One academic critic: voice aspires *to*, stops short of, light, music, silence. No word on *from*.

De profundis: under one ground, always another, always deeper. Under unfathomable *silence*, posit a third realm. It may be that not-here, there, elsewhere; above, below, or all-around which is both.

Realm of voice: the *vocal*. Speech (*parole*), idiolect of self in self-other reciprocity. Self allows of existence of other; other of self. While the voice is going-on, necessary illusion of the going-on never interrupted: *poésie ininterrompue, ininterrompable. Process* in its flight cannot fall back. The going-on is in the *newly-said*, essence of life, of immanence. Here, all is originality; however many voices there are together here, each one is unique. At least that is the myth of the vocal. The Maya prayer rises, interminable, idiolect of the particular shaman, grafted onto tradition but distinct, out of the one-and-only-heart. Any *other* shaman (in "my" place at least) must wait his/her turn.

Place. Call it the *nature* of a particular time/space: often a deity(ies) - pagan gods/goddesses of locality. Self and place talk to each other, reciprocally. Self: transient constituents of something believed to be I. Together with other selves: *culture.* Right here, in the *vocal*, that "original" self is mocked. Each constituent will have a voice in it; it will navigate through a sea of voices put out by other selves. Voices of each place, of each constituent of self, of each self, of each other, of each constituent of each other: self is never simplex. What is this voice-producing self? Reality? Illusion? Dispensable illusion? Necessary illusion?

Prospective Maya shaman follows his/her master. *Listens.* Again and again and again. No teaching as such. As in so many "primitive"/"archaic" situations: simply *being-with* the teacher; absorbing him/her, his/her one-and-only-heart-essence, by transmission. As you go deeper, it is not a one-and-only-heart but speaks with the dead (dead, pl.), may *be* the dead, below, above, out-there, returned here, in a new life, to the *vocal*. When you begin: a one-and-only-heart; in the middle: the many-hearted; at the end, the one-and-only-heart again.

While so much in the *vocal* teaches us the collective, our originality does not wish to heed it. All is subjective here, the collective is illusion. As illusion, it is displaced. Backward/downward: in which case, it is the myth of origin/presence/ logos/*arche*. Or forward/upward: in which case it is the classless society/ the end of history/*telos*. Call it if you like: lyric (forward); elegy (backward) [see NT on the Orpheus myth: *Substance*, no. 28, 1980].

Give the dead credit for some realitude: even as myth. Postulate, under silence, that not-here, there, elsewhere. Reverse the terms, what do you have? No-space/No-time: not a *place*, (it can be all-around). Non-reciprocity: self = other :: no-self = no other. Ambience of *langue*; *structure* (that from which *process* arises in optimistic flight, falls back into at each inevitable landing); the *already-said*; tradition (the *living* dead); transcendance. Call it the *choral*. In the *choral*, the *vocal* is illusion: all is objective, that is the *choral* myth. If the *vocal* is the locus of *poem*, the *choral* enwombs *page* or *text*: the possibility of all poetry/ all the possibilities of poetry/ all the poetries of possibility at all times, everywhere. [see NT, ibid, on the three aesthetics].

(The *living* dead: in Maya, as in so many "primitive"/"archaic" situations: distinguish the living-dead from the dead-dead. The living-dead are those who have had a deep effect on society, whose memory is, in effect, ineradicable, whose poetry is uninterruptible: who have had *social function*. These are the "returned"; in other traditions: the twice-born; the prophets risen live into heaven; the never-dead sleeping in caves; the once-and-future kings; the classics of the living lineages, not the dead crumblers of the academy. In the shamanic seance, I speak with the dead: those voices out there are the dead: I call them up to talk to us here.)

What about the middle-realm, the untalkative (no silent prayer in Maya: once you pray, you *talk*), the speechless, the *silence*? Realm of self-self reciprocity, of questioning. Closes everything off that's noise, allows *only* itself. Here *vocal* and *choral* can be thought to co-inhere - and who can challenge or question questioning, or question silence? If silence is a reality, it is perhaps the place where we question originality, you and I, and assign each one of us a due. Where we admit, in truth, what is already-said, what is newly-said - if we can ever tell them apart. Perhaps it is the place where we ask why that rush to the new is so fierce, that fall back to the old so crushing. Or come to terms both with the birth of lyric effervescence and the dying of slow settling elegy. Or see the one perpetually turn into the other as the cycle of *opus* comes alive. *Opus*: between individual *poem* and collective *text/page*, all the poems that the poet has written/ is writing/ will write in a lifetime. The poet's "prophetic" power, "shamanism": predicting forward lyric architectures; mining backward (nostalgic) elegiac archeology. Is *silence* an illusion or not: what do you say?

Or is the silence the sense we have that our poems are not, after all, given to us by our own pitiable, small-minded, restricted egos; that they are not virgin-born out of incest but truly engendered out of the marital air; that they are born with a task in the world, a mission here, a function, a purpose: that is, that *we* have something to do, to produce, to overcome, to stabilize, so that meaning might come into being word-in-word with our life?

In Maya, it is not that I am begging the world to act on my behalf; not that I am castigating it for not doing so - but that I am co-ercing it, word-in-word, word-after-word, both begging and castigating, ebb and flow of my prayer, setting it up in the voice, standing it up as the candles stand, as the gods stand, as everything stands and begins to dance.

With voice at the navel of earth and sky, navel of world, of living and dead.

E nihilo? De nada? Is this what we do down here?

Ombligo de Tesuque
XII.1.87

Voicing 25

Well, we all have our little ways...

Voiceprints=fingerprints, crimestoppers!

no two alike. (Added with characteristic
ploddingness).

So in part my anger at "voice-poetry" is that it takes one aspect
and fetishizes it, but it doesn't usually do that either --it takes a
"tone-of-the-time" semblance of voice...

Mind you, the Projectivists who developed
techniques--heck, who just wrote!
--using the practice of the person
met their times like a waterspout
and nailing it down as individual vs. abstracted soc'y
takes care of nothing. "Anyone" can read it
but not anyone can write it, only someone
who's going to die, like me.

So that "finding one's voice" generally speaking is a phrase
employed when the student has a set of tricks, trickles, like the
person who invented your videogame wasn't sounding much like
himself. "If sex were all, then any trembling hand."

Time goes, scar tissue forms and then
art has its announcements to make to itself
and that Person is no longer there
so new outfits need to be found.

No longer objects but systems.
After a [n un] certain point it ceases to
be a question of good or bad. If the motor's
going it's pumping the sump but she can no
longer recognize that sound, so small among
others irrelevant to the matter in hand.

I don't care for the stasis, don't believe it, it's not what I know,
one stage all one's life. The desk is more interesting for having
belonged to a woman who no longer had use for it who got it at
an antique store. That things come into
our hands is more interesting to me than to hang their simulacra
singly from the flies.

Personally, I don't think it's a matter of do away with voice (*voice*,
VOICE) --we need to see it's most of it bound to be
boring, because that's what we in this soc'y do to one another.
Commuting on the [un] freeways. That's boredom and we made it.

So I go to these readings and that old singsong
starts in--half rapt, half-assed--Thank God
for the shining exceptions, the formed intensities.

What's the occasion? Entranced intonings might prove appropriate.
It's not that there is (clearly there is) voice (= consistency of
diction and tone and content and concern) but that we are
voicements, voicings, voiced by language. And can vouch for this.
Laundry-lists maybe not, but towels were a breakthru, but then
everyone had spent a night at the Sheraton-Palace, or is it now
the Sheraton- Hilton. So some of us threw in not only the towel
but the bathroom fittings and the roach hotel and others drew the
gestures of throwing. That's all mere content, by now. It's what
you get when you unwrap the box that counts-- the enlightenment,
how baffling! You probably already HAD one of those.

I've said it all before and I'll say it again. Voice commonly means
that one aspect of the self has been hypostatized and so what
gets known as voice-poetry is a reactionary, defensive measure.
With what's exposed is the rest defended, even from oneself. It
selects from a single plane and there, as Olson said, It loses me,
it isn't the going-on I know.

They miss the art in it. It's all craft like stuff in Carmel. They
suppose Williams, Whitman and Wordsworth really spoke like that.
Then all you have to do is cut it into lengths and employ one of
several stitches. These are figures for apprehension. People...but
what do I know about people? I think, don't want to admit to
distance so miss distancing.

It doesn't matter about how many times I say I. It does what I
asks you to come up and watch him doing. It's not so simply
bourgeois of me to aver art's the bottom line. There is stupidity,
and there is blessed intelligence as in, news. Stupidity is ultimately
bad politically. We don't have to agree...

So what can you make of yourself?
Other languages /voices would extend
you, get *you* out of "yourself." --July /87

VOICE VOICING VOICES

I lost my direct access to the pages of the **Voice** when I had a fight? impassioned conversation with Alexandra Anderson, the art editor at the time. I lost contact with the **Voice** a couple years later when Carol Bovoso and Guy Trebay agreed to announce a boycott of G. E. as part of a Halloween poetry reading in support of the Plowshares 8. The **Voice** is a business.

It was their lawyers, as Frank Sinatra might say. It was also the end of me as a journalist, an impersonal teller of how it is. I had been an art art critic for six years, following a stint as a film critic, and an M.A. at Chicago and a Ph.D. at Columbia, both in contemporary poetry. I was column b for the **Voice**, David Bourdon, being column a. I was regularly getting bumped for ads. I dared to write about a coup in Peru and God at Niagara Falls, but politics was not my beat, they told me.

About this time, well before she'd published a line of poetry, let alone famous novels, Louise Erdrich told me how disappointed she was when buying a copy of **Mad**, she couldn't read it. I told her that **Mad**'s market was 12--16, as the **Voice** market was 16--25. I wasn't writing for the right market segment. Louise was about 22. We slept in the same bed like brother and sister. Now that's personal. The **Voice** of Greenwich Village is impersonal; everything has to be checked by a lawyer. Why? Murdoch, the **Voice** owner, has started a fourth network, FOX. The Unpuzzled Fox Foundation, Ltd., is a similar though not-for-profit corporation. G.E., destroyer of the Hudson River, maker of the MX-missle, owns N.B.C. Unmuzzled Ox hasn't got a grant in 7 years. Someone told me they read in The Village Voice that OX and *Cover* were vetoed by a Reagan appointee as political rather than literary. I haven't read *O.ARS* in years because it publishes an ex-wife. My lover said I shouldn't allow anything about my semi-affair with Louise to be published. I once wrote a book called *Fuck the Jesuits*. My mother told me not to publish it: the cover was done, a Mike Metz sculpture of a cross. I told my mother that the Jesuits wouldn't hurt me, the Rev. Dan Berrigan SJ was a personal friend. Nevertheless I heeded her words.

Poetry is spoken prayer to a personal diety. The dead are silent. I had an affair with Mary Gordon, before my first marriage; Mary and I were students at Columbia. Mary's second novel *The Company of Women* turns on an argument about the Rev Dan. The Rev Dan embraces Vatican II. This is the Age of AIDS. People don't have affairs. People masturbate; yet sales of girlie magazines are down, because people know masturbation really fans the flames of desire. The second millenium is coming, and we trinitarians hope there will be a third: we hope there will not be atomic war. Me, I kiss and tell. That's my voice, blabbing: only God can forgive, only He can judge.

one sd:

                              of rhythm is image
                              of image is knowing

                                                  the *body* itself as, by movement of
                                                  its own tissues, giving the data of,
                                                  depth

an imago of the insides, v. out
viz., t.v. (henceforth the *surround*)
which the Ols, although he did eventually break with and buy one,
condemned as, simply, one of "the 4 plagues of our time"

as if one could, in fact, walk
right past Dan Rather
into the Second Millennium. Maybe he could, the Ols
but back here on Charles Street, precisely
two blocks from the apartment he once inhabited, the conversation rarely turns
to Norse or with any specificity any other mythology. And when it does I run like
hell (cf. "Jung Food," *Freud's Own Cookbook*, Hillman and Boer, eds.). One has to
assume that the sacred territory is closed. Or, and which is much the same thing,
that Jung's flying mandala *does* land in just about everybody's back yard. The
problem is that the initiate may just decide to board it--and worse, then phone in
with the details like somebody ought to make a movie out of it.
     You laugh. But if the proposition stands that one does carry--and I hesitate
to say it--one's familiars

we might as well all pack our bags for Zurich.
That or save the fare, turning "to leftward,"
to that cavity, i.e., the body itself, in which
the organs, heart or "Mother," brain of "Father," liver or "Sister/Brother"
are, as Olson put it, "slung" as the corporeal points of origin of the
archetypes--and there is no doubt that the man was serious. The scheme
does not fare any worse at least than Jung's "psychoid substrate," but from
the lay perspective it is difficult to see that the dream personae--and that is where
the action is after all--have any visible means of support other than each other.
And the several and overlapping intrigues in which each may be involved. In other
words, it may not matter where, outside of the narrative domain peculiar to each,
the archetypal figure ultimately resides--or, rather, *dissolves*. What matters is the
body of lore, polymorphous, perverse, that may (or not) grow up around them. The
likely story. That, at least, is what Hillman and the gang seem to be saying (The
Myth of Analysis, The Dream and The Underworld), and if we add to our reading
list Derrida's seminal "Freud and the Scene of Writing"

     *For if there is neither machine nor text without psychical origin, there is no
     domain of the psyche without text.*

then we are out of the ontic altogether
and onto, at last, the page
as indistinguishable from "speech"
that is in Lacan's sense as that which gets floated like a bad check in the gap

between analyst and analysand, and securing the bond between them, so long as they both agree to the terms.

So. Rereading Freud we learn that *the unconscious is structured like a language.* The dream is a sentence, in both senses of the word--or as Freud had it, the dream is a kind of rebus or picture puzzle, its interpretation a matter of discovering beneath the image the word to which it alludes. What begins in language ends in language--or to put it quaintly, in a text that remains in a constant state of revision. And that mom and dad, the primal lovers, lurk behind our own inadequate attempts to reenact the horrible scene, that one is somehow fraudulent to begin with, having been chased out of childhood by what has become a Gorgon"s head on which we may no longer gaze--all that suffice it to say, was *his* story. Pure science. And a bit of a letdown. Fortunately, the dramatic potential of this initial text was not lost on Jung who revised "discontents" to read "Dis contents" by adding the anima and the animus, shadow, senex, puer aeternus, etc., to the cast of characters, thereby opening the god game to just about anybody, as it turns out, who wants to play. He even wrote a paper on flying saucers, but it is probably best to leave that one, as apparently Jung himself did, alone. I assume that the New Age types among us will vaporize of their own accord. But for those of us who lag behind it may still be considered a gain that from the standpoint of the unconscious, as if that made any sense at all, the *personal* has been replaced by *personnel*, the ego relativized, as it were, by the internal personae to which it suddenly found itself subservient. As King Pentheus, for one, learned the hard way--or how was it so many a Greek hero found himself at one point or another in drag? One might say, too, that the literature had become available, that is to amateurs like myself--a happy circumstance that Lacan & co. seem to be in the process of rescinding

The myth monger replaced by the word processor. From its nineteenth century beginnings as a secret retort of repressed contents (faculty psych through Freud, or the idea that nothing gets into the brain unless it first entered through eyes, nose, ears--a bias Freud never entirely shook off), through Jung's sacred and inherited preserve (the share), the unconscious migrates to its current resting place, viz., the page where, surprise, we find that it tends to submit to the rules of language. For the sake of argument. It shakes out that Jung, for all the criticism he had to endure for being, supposedly, an obscurantist or mystic, who at least managed to free the dramatist personae of the unconscious from the domain of the family romance and the literalisms to follow (Adler, Reich), and in so doing placed the individual in the middle of a narrative that had as many twists to it, at least potentially, as the various Greek, Egyptian, Orphic--whathaveyou--melodramas in which one might find equivalents. Unfortunately, it hath shook out as well that those equivalents are all too easily found (inflation), the dreamer identifying with the dreamed (Joseph Smith or Jim Jones, for that matter)

despite what Jung himself said on the subject, viz., that the gods and goddesses inhabiting the dream are, and in some ways precisely, what we are not.

And the narrative, if confined to nothing elsebut world lit in translation, does tend to volatilize which is why we began with, of all people, Olson and this curious insistence of his that it is the body itself cradles the unconscious and all that it might have in store for us

because in this way he would contain our enthusiasm, grounding it, as it were, in acts ("sitting down" or otherwise) actually performed

From a Letter to Charles Bernstein

Dear Charles:

I seem forever to be writing on Bastille Day. [Concerning 'voice'] actually, with whatever interest I in fact do have, I really found nothing to write or think about it. I could perhaps think in some other dimensional terms about 'voice' but I'm not at all sure it would pertain. As to say: 'Gift' for instance solves certain problems of 'engaged/disengaged' more appropriately than Creeley's "poetry as the only grace we may have in the chaos." The latter seems determinedly against determining what 'voice' (or gift) might be. But thinking here, couldn't it be that the 'gift' is a usefully "reversed" embodiment of Desire, enacting (actively) a plane of *availability* upon which it (and form) play out the themes of engagement (socious/sociality)? The gift could then be said to *form* the actual field of availability and action (as well as the 'emotive availability' that seems so central to poetry being predicated at all). The gift would be Desire's objectification, enacting form by a reversal of its socially coded fact. (That would be an interesting reading of Royet-Journoud.)

For example, I am interested in that huge middle area, which is neither the 'real' nor imagination, but something which we tend too easily it seems to call phenomenal. But if Spicer was insistent on anything it was upon the equality radio and message, not their equivalence, but corresponding enactment. So lets go further and talk about desire and realize that the radio makes the Sender existent in a very fundamental way. Cast into a different dimension, closure is local and never global; that the set of priorities by which to decide upon which sub-set is 'true' in the global field of possibles is an impossible set; the lack of a transcendental fact denies the possibility or efficacy of any election of a so-called meta-set. However, closure on a local level is *necessary* for any intelligibility. 'Fact' is perpetually in conflict with 'truth' (knowledge). Assuming either outright is a powerful antidote to agency, as I think Ollie North has demonstrated. A multiplication of overviews solves nothing. The welter of targets deranges ones self-generated perceptivity, it's true. But that only complicates things, doesn't finally deliver the exaction necessary if words, lines, are to yield, together with the speed or momentum they are capable of, a meaning beyond the individuals each polity is continually breaking up into.

But the question (esp. considering this issue of 'voice') might be: If I discern, with excitement, the line breaking up into its accessed singularity, then why object? The solution seems to concern the noumenal/phenomenal split in the model I'm urging. Naturally, we need those bits, facts, accessible shards of the 'real'. But equally I insist upon an overarching global dimension, as undemonstrable as that may be. The negation here is double: Debris as a category describes a simultaneous that is 1. the breaking free from dominance of the global, loaded as it will be with ideological scum, and 2. the negation then of that isolateness, self-consciously, a reflex that is not necessarily the work of this, that, or any particular writing. (This might well be the argument against 'voice' --dissenting perhaps *from* Olson while making the strongest possible argument for him, and particularly for his overall project, again what Barry [Watten] calls 'method'.)

Let me come in another way: When Rosmarie Waldrop was here (some time ago) she made an argument for the writing of Albiach and Royet-Journoud, which, although apparently appropriate, didn't in the end convince me that any of us had really solved this question. Fundamentally, she followed Jacobson's "axis of selection projected onto the axis of combination" argument, pushing the point that current poetry, at least French poetry had obviated the metaphor, image, etc., all that baggage of the vertical (selection) axis, opting now for the total metonomy of the other. Obviously this leaves us in the quintessentially local domain. But what if I can discern a *trajectory of metaphor* that is neither one nor the other, but of both the vertical and the horizontal, that does not embody or represent the non-dynamic systemic qualities of the vertical, but rather dynamizes them. It seems to me that Peter Middleton's excellent article on narrative in *Poetics Journal* #5 argues just such a model as 'narrative' and it seems that a similar insistence upon a dynamic crossing of axes within any writing is what solves the dilemma. And again this comes back to noumena/phenomena. That is, it seems to me that a dogmatic insistence on 'process'(the refusal to edit, the insistence upon the improvisatory, etc.) binds work within, as Bachelard says, "romantic or humanist prejudice against science." I'm much more interested in the notion of revelation as it comes out of ideas like Barry's "fundamental investigation" or Bachelard's own idea of "englobement."

7/14/87

/*Paul Buck*

approach now through the outgrowth textures
through the obstacles of apparitions the consolidation of
ideas of vocalization through cries of desire that have to dodge
lift swells to search loaded with an
anticipated surging feast filled with jumps at the sexual
here too the skill possible to detach
draw the passion from the compressed self melting
perform to texts to hook desire through
certain sensations of the body
many tinctures emphasizing some of its lines
terrain living but especially fissures and mouths
down through ever-renewed oral memories
simply their order of occurrence after that
delight of the terrain distance between variable catches
certain residues
insistent impassioned is this wrong other modes of compulsion
confront a continuous dialog until the temples
metamorphose the sounds compose a particular piece
slowly erect on the steps

Voicing 32

to procure an insight whilst becoming the whitening
motions appearing and vanishing this is where
the unfolding of itself is whispered
sounds that memory bares paralyzed
explicit and provokes the least functional aspect
where fractures summon up even encourage a performance
loosen the mask of the trembling confront aches for the appetite
permeate the aggressive elbows and challenge imagined contrivance
together one cannot speak rooted by the violent pull of ground swell
these matters are regarded as sacred costs us guilt interest
gloves in this pursuit would be pointless
repulsion there is the admission for various disguises
reconstruction of an earlier fountain of trials
two tries which are torments distinct outside of pillows

the purpose the attempts are meant to modulate on this support
used as a basis for moments of attraction and succession among
the distortions of tradition rather than their irregularities
gleaned from them and the extension handles
among other passionate vocalizations include the penetration of its agony
delayed strengths another arousal that can articulate display moved
and the search for humor insufficient for combustion
increase exhalation where surface stresses appear
dread appears in the main combustion is
the use of trembling using the extreme
more than indicate the obsession to attribute to such leverings
to follow ideas step by step

Aboriginal Voicing

STATEMENT AND COUNTERSTATEMENT

Learning how to read means learning how to hear sound inside oneself--a strange ability if you come to think about it. For me, the sound of the poem = the "hollar" in my shout about the pleasured most, not echoed off any previous, not sounded by being heard out loud. A phraseology of busted moods & statement music, murmured in the liquor of a frozen thought.

COUNTER-STATEMENT ON VOICE

"Voice" first of all makes me think of--not just the great ones but also those who made their music in the din of the radio & who are now drowned out in the static of time--Sonny Til & "Pookie" Hudson, Eugene Record (author of "Oh Girl," one of the sweetest songs ever to grace Top 40), Gloria Jones, Lee Dorsey--there have been literally hundreds.

When I think of poetry as music--not just the sound of the words but also the "singer" those words seem to demand we be--I wonder if voice works even as an approximate description. In a funny way, there's no real reason to think of the sounds that words demand *in* us (not the sound *we* make when we speak them) as vocal. After all it wasn't the songs that made Bessie Smith empress of the blues--"torn hurdygurdy lithographs of dollfaced heaven" that those songs may have been, to quote Robert Hayden--it was what she did with them.

To me, what a poem does is articulate a sound in which it's possible to make statements that *may* communicate themselves to a reader--something all musicians do, not just singers. It may be that "voice" and "language" are distinct media, just like "voice" and "piano."

"Inside [Dolphy's] sound," Charles Mingus once said, "was a great capacity to talk ... We used to do that you know. We used to actually talk in our playing." When I think of the sound of language in poetry, I think of favorite singers but I also think--especially lately--of instrumentalists. I think of Lester Young, whose solos were said to follow intonations suggested by the lyrics, & I think of Eric Dolphy (the squawk of his solo on Mingus' "Bemoanable Lady"). I think of gut-bucket players like Big Jay McNeely who honked and screamed their one note riffs with the same abandon you hear when Little Richard sings "Tutti Frutti" or Jerry Lee Lewis shouts "Great Balls of Fire"--& I think of players like Cecil Taylor & Ornette Coleman, whose inimitable sounds critics invariably describe as self-contained languages.

But here the question of how poetry relates to music gets technical & and I get in over my head. Pop a beer and listen up. Walkover to the stereo and flip the record ...

MONK

Thelonius Monk made the piano a theatrical space, a theatre, endowing it with volume, depth, shadow, vanishing perspectival points, and wings. "In the wings" of Monk's theatre you hear the occasional heavy sounds of people moving furniture (Max Roach's timpani in "Brilliant Corners"): the stage hands of such artistry are the adepts of harmonics (Rollins especially), initiates of Ellington's harlem airshaft (Coltrane said working with Monk was like falling down an elevator shaft: think of Charles Laughton, racing to escape, prying open the elevator door to his doom in "The Big Clock"--this is when Trane learned to fly!) taking wing.

Listen to "Well You Needn't" in the 1957 date with Trane. After his bluesy chorus Monk barks out "Col-trane Col-trane" and sets up an entry so deftly and sparely that, for the first four or five bars, you can actually *hear* Coltrane's *hesitation*. Monk gave him pause. Not intimidation, but a difference in the space of hearing, the acoustic residuum of tact. ((And then, later in the same take, listen to Blakey's growling gusto, the hurricane unleashed--that what Monk favored among sidemen was rhythmic exuberance, not harmonic boast.))

With Monk every temporal node yields a complete geography. Fitting the hands to the keyboard is akin to a surveyor placing the tripod for a measurement. Distance, span, plane, and incline are relevant terms.
Inclination.

Monk: someone grumbling aloud in his sleep, turning over. A gymnast of somnambulation. *Mn mn mn.*

In Monk's music every phrase as played˙ is a rhythmic cell. And each cellular inclination smuggles some harmonic contraband into the picture, across the border and past the zone of the dimwit foot-tap indifferential. Prismatic alliances are formed.

With Monk, as in Webern, you never know the exact measure being applied, so you don't "see" the size of the object that, in a system of representation, would figure into the calculus of a 'ground.' With some of his pieces you don't know whether the 'tune'--and you might not be able to say what *that* is--is the skin or the bone of the event. Whether it holds up and constitutes the internal structure horizon, or whether instead (as in Roland Barthes' erotic principle of hermeneutics, interpretation's like peeling layers off an onion: there's no core, no seed, no bottom, just an *end to onion*--as in the one about the world perched on the back of an elephant...and what's the elephant standing on? A turtle. And the turtle? Why, it's *turtles all the way down!*) every figural motivation is an excursion not distinct in principle from a series of steps, bends, twists, none of which are ever done with any sort of calculation of their place in a finite series. Every gesture is the infinitude within the moment of its release.

With Monk, it's all denotation, no connotation. The most classically pianistic music since Haydn. The plectrum of the cogito: fingers drumming the edge of a table. Or the edge of a seat during a lecture, hearing not the analytical persuasion of the talk but the budgeting of sidesteps, tones, the *largo* of the drawl, the crunch of its release. The size of the footprint.

Because Monk's music is rhythmically propagated, one can't speak of "details" or embellishments of his style. Is there any other pianist for whom this would be the case? The grace notes are all down there, nose to the ground, canine.

Monk's tunes are the propositional counterparts of a labyrinth. Getting in and getting out again are what it's all about. Crossing raging waters. Monk's own pianistic applications disclose the essential survival tools. He plays not according to predetermined rhythms, but as someone crossing a river, stone by stone. There is the hesitation, the creative preparation, the foresight--followed by a contagion of leaps, clustered, bippety-bip-bip, bop, budobbopp. Are your cuffs wet? Yet?--they will be. Monk's music is like learning to roll with the fall. A keyboard full of 'good sportmanship.' A metronome coming undone or unwound. Being 'wound up'--tense or nervous--is the antithesis of everything Monk's about. Cooling out tension's what he's after. In pop-song format the "bridge" of the AABA 32-bar framework is also known as the *release,* the *inside* or the *channel.* Think of a floodgate, listening to Monk: a volume of liquid pressed against a restraint, then suddenly released. Monk's mastery of voice: *to compose the release.*

---

as played: Even "Tea for Two" on the Ellington set demonstrates the principle as handily, that it's Monk's style of playing that precedes and makes itself its own avant-garde in advance of the compositions. Or put it another way: it's the compositions that *advance the style.*

/C.D. Wright

GIG EM:

experta credita illegitimati non carborundum

Where we have unloaded the car for the month of July --between Lead Hill and Peel, Arkansas-- twenty minutes down an ungraded dirt road, the trees encroach on the road, weeds fill in the would-be median, monarchs or viceroys extravagate in front of the windshield. An indefatigable variety of spider twills web after web across the car's path. A roadrunner keeps a few jerky feet ahead of us.

The cabin is in view of the lake which lies below us like a gigantic slab of lapis. The cabin comes completely equipped, including trash compactor. When we step onto the deck, indigo buntings are flushed out of the oaks. I brought along Thoreau, promising myself to read him through this time, but I also brought along Robert Schole's *Textual Power,* and after an hour on the scratchy couch with Thoreau, I am on the linoleum with Scholes. Thoreau, as it turns out, did not scratch my itch. Today's itch, July 3.

The first night is spent in fear. We make a brazen effort to frighten the spiders back, out of the house. The crickets and cicadae commence their crepitations. Then come the owl and whippoorwill, bullbats, bullfrogs; the trolling motors and country and western stations. I hate country music. It's my culture, so to speak, so I can hate it if I want to. However, we can pick up NPR from Point Lookout, MO at The School of the Ozarks. Likewise I disapprove NPR. It is increasingly compromised and more and more given over to trifling features that displace an already compromised point of view. More belly-up liberalism. NPR's token poet is Andre

Codrescu. He produces a spray of cultural ephemera laced with Transylvania-style red-baiting via Baton-Rouge. Bad breathed and fanged. And no cultural watchdogs from anyone within 3000 miles of the left. I think of three immediately: Gore Vidal, Hunter Thompson, and Ron Silliman. Even me, right off the chittlin circuit. A rash of bromidal diarists represent our most dilatory prose. Now they are serializing a Hell's Kitchen M.D.'s memoir. Utterly bland, patrician. And while a sixty-second spot might be allotted a Greenpeace organizer, a lengthy interview will be given Pat Buchanan with no reference to his true identity as chief extremist strategist for Nixon as well as Reagan. No mention of the innumerable frauds he perpetrated on the public in order to guarantee a lasting, far-reaching, far-right regime. Pat Buchanan the well-regarded Goebbels of our darkening day, who by a modicum of applied existing law would be wearing a number on his uniform for many eclipsing days to come. Comes a point, Brotherettes and Sisterettes, you just twist the knob to the left and tune the insects in. You pray they prevail. "Blessed are they who never read a newspaper..." I hear you now Henry.

Town --with just under ten thousand souls-- provides an uplifting intermission. The sign at the city limits reads, **Jesus Is Lord Over Harrison And Surrounding Area**. And **Surrounding Area** appears on a second signboard, affixed perhaps on second thought to underscore the extent of His Reign. I am sure the signmaker's ambitions were not to create a limited sovereignty. But there you have it. More signs on the fringe: **Learn Hell Is Hotter** cautions a church marquee; **GAR** remains over a defunct garage while a customized car plate urges, **GIG EM**.

With the advance of telephone poles I am borne up. At the station we fill the tank with unleaded, then pay. The most minor purchase is treated as an intimate transaction, can give rise to a life history. People are plain interested in you and they want to tell you where they were stationed whawl they wuz in the service or when they wuz young n crazy. They want to tell you about somebody praktikly biting their ha-ed off when they asked di-rekshuns up there or else about an unexpected kindness done them when they run unto trouble. And they have information to burn: Ho-made creme pie can be had at.... But it is not what is said or the adages splattering everything said like ketchup; it is the acoustics I care about. I may hate country music, but give it to me acapella, unscored, uninhibited by an audience of one, and I am rapt. I am a re-born believer in country speech. Jonathan Williams has been quoted saying, he has turned more and more away from the high art of the city for what he could unearth and respect in the tall grass. Unimproved poetry is an expression I have come to appreciate.

Here is why: Even beautiful Santa Fe has a Wal-Mart regardless of the Council's clout in keeping it on the outskirts. And in Harrison, AR, alongside the rest of the homogenized commodities, the Esprit line is available within days after the label's latest California release. In other words our alleged culture is not only agressively uniform, but also instantaneously so. Ponder this: the best of the statewide Arkansas dailies (the newest link in the nefarious Gannett chain) runs a wire photo of a *young entrepreneur* from Quincy, MA retailing Ollie For President t-shirts on the street. Didn't we once call this sales force *teenage*, and their methods *hawking*. The accompanying article provides Ollie's legal assistance address on the chance readers want to send in their dimes and dollars. In fairly recent times didn't we call this a *free political advertisement* not *front page news*. No matter. I am nearly beyond insisting words have meaning apart from the speaker's intention. For here, for now I just want to make the modest claim that voices have character inherent to their aural qualities. And that character maintains a next-of-kin relation to art; it is the matrix of *difference*.

If the opinion-shaping industries have successfully colonized our[*] minds to the

---

[*] *our* meant broadly and including "us" poets as voting and non-voting citizens, not as an otherwise determinate sect.

point that the so-called alternative airwaves are taken up with scarcely veiled red-baiting, then a poet should indulge her senses for signs of a difference, a subversion. Asked by the overalled man selling watermelons off the gate of his pick-up, "You want a stripe-ed melon or a solid un," a poet should waste no time in getting out her coin purse for the stripe-ed. To know which is sweeter you would have to buy both. But to choose you need only to favor the acoustics of one over the other. What I favor is the persistence of a *difference.* Since decades of TV and radio have not yet managed to wipe out these distinctions, I am inclined to believe they can survive. At some level, Will is at work, because at some level more than a mere hidebound accent is at risk. There is a refusal to be bought out by The Chain, more so with the disappearance of Trust not to mention anti-Trust. A dis-Willingness to render unto The City what belongs to The Country. A cranky tone, a defiant attitude, an underlying rhythmic thump of the foot distinguished those who go to bed with the chickens from those who go at none o'clock. On this matter the chickens are equally dependable. Autochthons have their own sound, notes that go with the sound. THat's what I listen for.

Living, temporarily, at the end of this road we wear our digitals out of habit but refer to them less and less. We go to bed when we feel like it. If we seek an intermission from the din of insects we can go to town for ho-made pie. Banana creme or ka-ro nut. Ice cream, one dip er two.

Speech Sheet

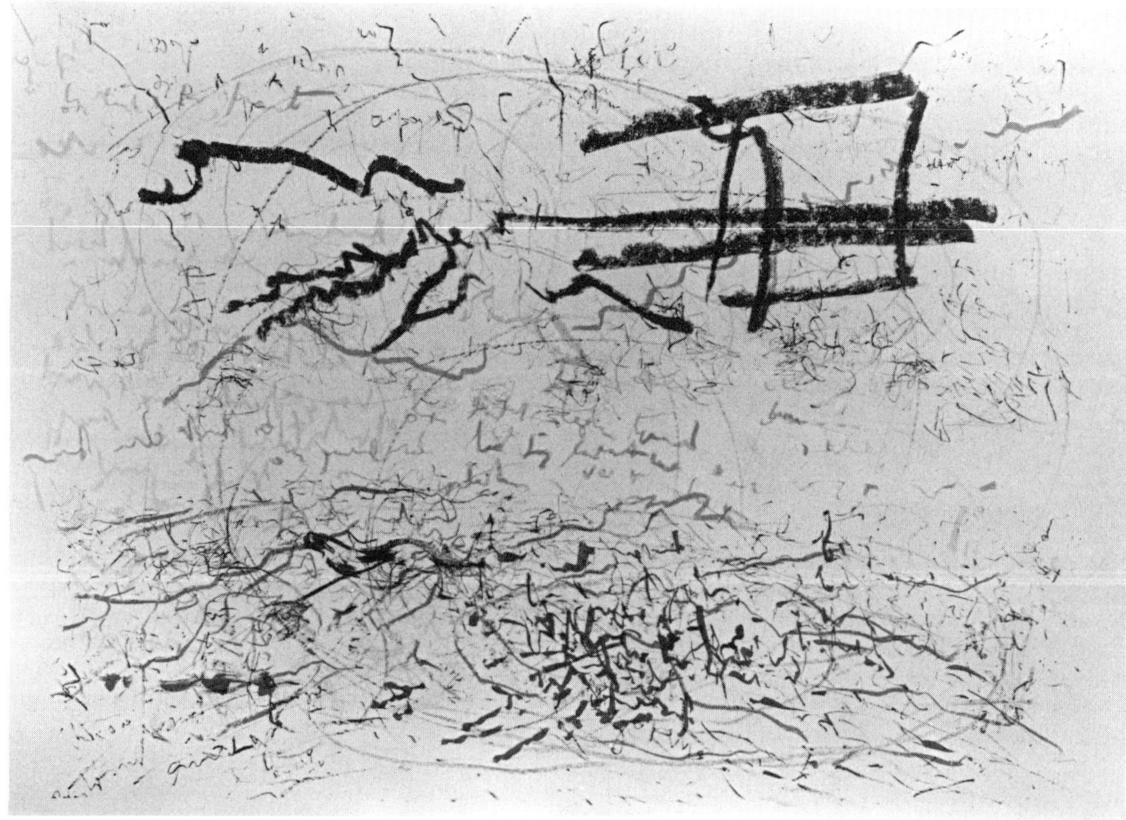

Carl Friedrich Claus, *Denkatmosphäre 1978-82*

WHO'S SPEAKING PLEASE?

Notes on Voicing:

Voice is an integral term in the relationship of a person to language. For instance, "Voicing" describes the activity of a speaker by modulating, directing and framing a speaker's address in a specific occasion. "Voice", however, is a signifier identifying an individual language user. In this sense "voice" loses its primacy and takes on distancing characteristics which in turn redefine or replace a message with personality.

The problematic aspects of this shift from "voicing" to "voice" are particularly evident in the role of voice in written work. In writing, the primacy of oral speech is subjugated to the tyranny of the printed page; the speaker is absent, and has been replaced by a text. "Voice" is a term, particularly in poetry, for stylistic devices which represent an identity. The voice in the text is a personalized animation of language that "stands for" the speaker. The activity of voice in this context is to produce style which subsequently becomes a dominant content of the work. The specificity of a direct address is repressed by the power of genre, device and social convention.

The restoration of voice to an integral primacy in the relationship of language and address may proceed on a variety of levels. For instance, it may be suggested that language *means* and voice *measures*. Nevertheless, meaning is inherent in measure and carries a content, if not always a reference system, that is as important as other aspects of language. The question of person and address, of the speaker speaking, is central to the way voice conditions meaning.

In the traditional relationship between writer and text, the writer assumes a focal, though invisible (or in this case inaudible) role and gives voice to language in the form of shifting devices, such as characters or narrators. The writer mediates between different conditions and occasions of language. This process allows for two related concepts of voice: the writer's "voice" as style, and the presented voices of the writer's devices, including the character "I" which might or might not represent the writer. Both are conditioned by the restraints and codes of the address system in which language is treated as vehicle rather than material.

An alternate practice might establish the materiality of language and/or voice by enacting a situation in which the writer is a conductor of language which originates somewhere else. Jack Spicer declared himself a receiver and transcriber of outer voices. Hannah Weiner represents the flashing circuits of language crossing her mind as diverse voices speaking to or through her. Jackson MacLow, among others, employs external procedures to construct texts which are often collaged from found sources, each of which might be considered a "voice". These writers locate the speaking voice within the operations of writing. The speaker is apparent as a silhouette, a negative presence, against a blinding light of "external" language.

To unite a speaker/writer with the formative activity of voicing, voice must be presented as a conditional, active term, rather than as a representation of style or language. The presentation of a primary voice as a contextualizing device solved the problem of the artifice of the written text for Samuel Beckett. In *The Unnameable* a disembodied voice directly addresses and questions, without further convention or description, the occasion of its speaking. The "speech" of the book stammers, contradicts, and generally develops within the frame of a voice "voicing". David Antin, who's dealt with this dilemma even more directly, has given up the artifice of writing on the page for works that are oral improvisations for specific public occasions. These works are later transcribed, edited and published as documentation of an event. Other writers, including many in this volume, have made performance requirements integral to their written work so that comprehension requires a voiced reading. In Antin's talk pieces, through a recognizable device in Beckett, and by a specific performance requirement in diverse other work, voicing occupies the first level of the text, and establishes the literal presence of the speaker.

The context in which voicing occurs serves to unite a speaker with the object of his/her discourse, that is, a listener. As the speaker speaks, a listener listens; the voice of each is indistinguishable from the other. The speaker is part of the listener, recognized or constructed by another language act, regardless of the seeming "otherness" of the speaker. Writing which attempts to establish such "direct" address foregrounds this relationship within the act of voicing.

Unlike language constructed on or for the page, the terms of speech are uniquely immediate, open, fluid and sited in the experiential world. Printed representations of speech-based works attempt to foreground their textual status in the context of performance notation and/or documentation and thereby link the reader to an active and specific occasion of voice. In the vapor of this exchange, voice is again a sound, a presence, a music; and the speaker is a gesture, an act constantly moving toward itself.

Body Poetry Notation:

TEASING RELEASE

Jean-Paul Curtay
from *Teasing Release*
(O.ARS 7, *Translations C,*
1985).

INTRODUCTION*

The vision seeks the man.
---Zora Neale Hurston

I came to jazz just as I was.

In the beginning, it is a matter of supplication to be made a member of the sanctified church. Later it becomes the discovery, an apparently enabling discovery, of an informing source for poetry. Still later it becomes a prolonged and perhaps not to be released from encounter with the sirens, both their song and the aftermath--bones among a field of flowers--of their song. I use the sirens as a figure for my encounter with the voice and with one of its primary instruments, the horn. There are other instruments, but in this area of decision, in the sanctified church of jazz, the horn is primary. A matter of supplication becomes a question of survival. What is to be survived is the power, the face-eating power to the third power of the voice.

Not knowing the power of the voice, I asked for the wrong thing. To ask to be made a member of the church is to ask for the wrong thing. When, in time and in the circle of repetition, I came to the knowledge of the voice, there was nothing but the stench of terror. To ask to be made a member is to ask for the wrong thing. What is to asked for is how to stay alive.

The first jazz that made itself available to me was "The Drum Thing" on John Coltrane's *Crescent* album. It was a story, a narrative; it had something to do with a journey across a wide expanse. And it was with a journey or simply a straggling procession of musicians in mind that I began the poem. It's tempting to say the music gave me the poem. The contribution of the music, however, was more an instigation, a prompting to begin, than a complete template.

It was the first poem which truly pleased me. It seemed to exist apart from me, to have an object existence of its own. And I knew that, without the music of John Coltrane and Elvin Jones, it would have had no existence at all.

Helped in the on-going work of composition and protected from becoming a parasite of personality, the poet is pleased and happy. What more could be desired? This was my feeling in writing the later poems prompted by jazz. Ornette Coleman's "Lonely Woman" on his *The Shape Of Jazz To Come* album involved yet another journey across a wide expanse; and Lester Young's playing, whether with the smaller Kansas City groups or with the Basie big band, had a behind-the-beat poignancy that involved him in a pursuit by green meteors and other personages of the night.

I made a grid from the sheet music for "Lonely Woman." The idea was that my lines, shaped in compliance, might take on some of the rhythmic character of the music. Even as I did this I suspected it would not be enough to transpose

---

*   *From a manuscript of poems entitled* **Prompted by Jazz.**

already transposed music into poetry. There would have to be transformation. Not "jazz poems," my poems would have to start from and go away from jazz. They would have to end up somewhere else.

The music could be blues--what Ornette always plays and what tends to come through whatever the context Lester was playing in--, and the poems themselves could be elegiac occasions. In "Coming Forth By Day," the poem that takes off from Ornette, ponderous women move among the deaths of fire, air, and lands. In the Lester young poem, the death is Lester's own, but reconsidered as a night scene. The music could be blues, the poems could be elegiac, but I was pleased and happy. What I had yet to hear was the voice behind the music. What I had yet to understand was the relation of the music, the voice, and my own defacement.

Several years later, when "Giant Steps" was written, I still had not heard nor understood. What more could be desired? Jazz was my church, my informing source. And while I had gone on to listen to much more of it both before and after Coltrane, his music continued to be the center of my source. I had developed an unresting cadence, a cadence which in the motion of its going seemed to have certain affinities with his "sheets of sound." And, by way of etymological research into the terms of his titles, the potential vocabulary of the poems was enlarged. Through this cadence and vocabulary the potential of composition was enlarged and expanded.

I was a willing, eager supplicant in the church of jazz, and it continued through all its various promptings to lead me on.

I do not remember at what moment I began to hear and to understand. No doubt, it was a gradual, not prepared for much less sought after process. I thought I was writing poems that started from jazz and eventually got away from it. What I thought was wrong. By the time I came to write "Not Quite Parallel Lines" I knew what I had thought was wrong. Two musicians appear in the poem: Coltrane and Albert Ayler. They are cited as exceptional natures which I am heir to and which nevertheless must be opposed. There must be opposition because they are players--and thus are played through--of the horn of the voice.

Who would have dreamed these exceptional natures must be opposed? I hadn't and didn't want to. It seemed blasphemous to go against those I most admired, those who had prompted me to discover the potential of my own composition. What I gradually began to hear through them, however, was the animal power of the voice, what I gradually and reluctantly began to understand was that the power of the voice meant my own powerlessness.

Composition is attention. If jazz is its instigation, that means leaning and leaning in more intently in listening to be able to write. With more intent listening come admiration and love. At the same time the listener becomes increasingly vulnerable, exposed, to what plays through the players and their instruments. This is the voice which eats the face away. It is the voice which turns the face of the listener, member among the members, into its excrement.

Odysseus encounters the sirens once. The growing, undeniable intensity of admiration and love and the existence of recordings mean a constant encounter and re-encounter. In this circle of repetition there is always a call, there is always a being spoken to. *The vision seeks the man.* In the area of decision of jazz the members cannot help but to hear the call and what is being spoken.

Once having come to jazz, like language, there is no leaving. There is only the

trying to decide against being turned into the called and bespoken, there is only
the constant trying to decide to stay alive.

/John Taggart

COMING FORTH BY DAY

after a composition by Ornette Coleman

Cold and, cymbals fizz with no old animals among railroad tracks,
tarred   grass in   still   winter,
austral herons beating, beating grey ellipses over closed cities.

Ponderous women move as slowed film, the
chrome tendons in night, furious lengthening bar, broken within them,
them, intense anatomies' dark edges as eruptions along suns,
clouds, as interiors, heavier than oil, sediment on glass,
                                            grass tarred, gravel afire.

Women contain things as lighted signs apart
from the darkness, motionless, split, vibrating and without hope,
          air lives in   death of   fire.

The trees fronting the sea   are as fans, reversed, the
eastern harbor, ridges, backs of buildings in smoke,
water   lives in death of   air.

                                        Machines burn in zones of
pure aluminum. Alluvial plains with abandoned factories, upheaval,
fire lives   in death   of lands.

Ponderous women move out of frames, the
metal in palm trees, muscles, the hum of refineries no longer

them, and twisted grass the breasts with knees, ankles of black gravel,
Now, as mirrors, revolved, oiled with carbon, not holding
                                        old animals,   railroad tracks.

Women are as lighted signs in dancing, when
coming upon cities from regions of winter by day,

          birds fade out, rising.

Reprinted from Maps 1 (1966).

RUSHLIGHT-1

sun in eyes with the brush
  seven & then roll on eleven
    thickening viridian
thought we were hushed
  by the multinationals
    & their profitable trap
dealing portable breath
  products of us
    more were drawn
money razing & alterations
  mining the books
    each page
a landscape compressed for extraction
  crimson lake by favour of frost
    layers blotch neon dazzle
groan alley every sip from broken
bottles   passing shards
rebels carry off all corn & hay
  in the way from sterling
    fear the number of men
at night or in light
  of them at Autcherarder
    drove blue into eye
was lost in long reach
  last night a house fell
      down in shoe lane
at his leve
  quakes of retrenchments
    city on which bridge
can you stand
  watch leaders fade on screens
    flash interference
gutter resembles dry tongue
  in the street
    even fewer share the shares
night lingers in these bones
  river frozen so hard
  people pass daily purple
        & watermen build booths
          sell liquors therein
a printer set up a press
& publishes the names of several people

that they may tell they were printed
       upon the river
     as an ox whole will be roasted upon ice
     of their closeness
     come down capital
       loiters upon one another
     morning clouds
   seals from beyond seas
bounce of rainfall glistens shape
  hiding moon fearless
     languages of water
come in gush the growing
        of their flows
   of trees stretch next island
   to meet
     naming her
     sound to cove
       i love & care
engraved on every visual display unit
  from nuclear computers dancing teletext
      sapped in their bunkers
  arms lock on each aggressor
     the long wait in sights
       for themselves alarm
  when the glass cracks feel peace
     hoonah reef depths reflect in our eyes
       time the pulse pulses
       wagers froze at the edge
         any hand sucked
                        in the new deep
                        now full of ice
                where water was never known
                       the
                       thaw
                   being now
                 in blue light
authorities decisions disappear
                     open wings in crosswinds
                reaching tides ebb jade

9/1/86

I DO NOT SHARE BLOOD

I wish the flesh of me, bitten! --- till raw, and my mouth filled
with iron, or lead, or coin; I wish to vomit the coin. Oh read with
me, soft, or aloud, in this room, which is only the memory of a
room, a darkness, in which I sit, or have sat, my writing, or my-
self, being that record, and that sole danger, of invention, and
invented pause. *I do not share blood, for my body does not bleed*
---it is dry, and darkened by the infinities of nights, by the
infinities of clouds, and the infinities of stars, moons, and the
spaces between stars, moons --- the distances in which they die,
as if delved, or delivered, in dirt. I acknowledge myself; I
acknowledge a scratching, on paper, a hand, pinched on a pen; I
acknowledge what's read; I acknowledge ability, and lack of ability;
I acknowledge carnage; I allow the disgust, for terminus must
disgust. *The terminus; hell; fini* --- with what door, now? With
what door open? With what directing to dark? Should I abhor the
guest who is not here? Should I call her by name? Should I name
him, who is the meaning of her? There is the sublimity, of a
silence, which does not wreck itself with answers. If I say:
*There is a silence now that I would not add my hearing to, but
substract it from,* I am involved, not merely with a conditional,
but the striking out of a conditional. When there is silence,
there is a plural of silence. The mouth cocks itself sideways,
and screams into a sister-mouth. The mouth hears nothing. It is a
dead hole, an insufficiency that cultivates more insufficiency.
Were it a bladder, it would become a blooming of black. Were it
nothing more than an anus, it would seeks the communications of
a god.

1-2/9/86   (corrected 30/1/87)

PEN, THOUGH *PRAECIPE*

Pen, though *praecipe* --- in
lull, and traverse;   the
ends are prose, by position, like a
glory of a flower-head, or the closed
eye of a sleeper, for a day, or
an hour, in
eve, or dark. My
hand is writ, in fascination, for it
examples its permanence, and
locates its communion, of
power, in the welling up, of a
welcome --- or an
au revoir.   In the liberties, of
literacy, the elite moment may
eliminate the free.   If I
join in the *pourboire*, or
ovation, or to nip the rind of many
lemons, should I decry, or make,
light of, my want, or my rest, or my share?

5:2:86

PASTORAL INCURSIONS

Where neither way nor ground is clear words
     crop up again in new margins: the poll
steals a head less politic than fearfully polite,
     raked indirectly back in lawn order.

*

Raked indirectly back in lawn order Lord
     help us to go straight to the source
of confusion.   Light stumps ahead.   Because
     light stamps the ground, not a word.

*

Light stamps (not a word) the ground elder.
     Yesterday's broadsides flap across the lawn
and the margins of belief, too early to be warned
     not to look straight ahead, out of order.

*

Not to look straight ahead in the order words
     come in time to observe.   Light slips
through your hands or else the margin slopes
     both ways, untoward.

AN ELEATIC DIRGE FOR WILLIAM EMPSON

Vows are re-fashioned as the voice
dies out along the flight-path. The paradox
points back to the problem arrow.   The voice
dying out describes the view

whereas the view describes more than
the limits of the voice.   Reconnaissance looks
westward: renaissance dies out along
the flight-path.   Can I out-describe you

or you me?   It is the arrow on a map,
pointing west of the page, which the paradox
points back to. Isn't all time lost by definition?
It points back along the flight-path, re-fashioned.

REPETITION

The mirrors gave us reasoning:
this stranger must be me.

God of light who looks back
over the slow fields
the leaves rising to their pages
in the trees

Once was enough
to know the face of oblivion---
the empty carriage circles recklessly.

Hear the voice escaping from the branches,
no one waits for you in the glass.

January Sixth

Here white snow covers everything
and what it doesn't turns black against it.

This morning has that clarity, a sureness
in the eye, as clear-cut as animal tracks

Metaphysical Assumptions

A smell in the kitchen creates
elegant movements,

cumin, cinnamon, animals, and men
crossing white sands,

caravans of quiet evening,
perfumed continents of a cup

filled again, the tiny chip
where willows flank pagodas

beneath whose hills a boat glides,
and two birds mate mid-air

and three bent figures hurry
across a bridge at dusk.

Table

The perfection of
a blue bowl
of eggs

remains constant
in the mind, as simple

as clear
as a cold
glass of water

An Equation

The yellow air and earthly ox.
Unmade and grazing in the sun.

A knife, a block of olive wood.

Adam & The Alphabet

A spoken thing? A word--
a matter of tongue,
business of teeth:

the door, the house, the head, the hand.

Am I a man of words?
I am the man of things,

red, blue, wild, or otherwise:
The hand that is a door
the word that is a dwelling

Studies

How many levels constitute reality?
Or when is what is seen most real?

Yellow wax fruit, set upon a plate
the color of broth or pear trees.

Or a lemon because of the skin.

The Paragraph

A man throws out a net. To capture something?
Three times the call comes, not a curse.

He hands me a white rose.
"These knives cut that dark very well."

On a highway at night the car stalls.
A cat scratches my arm. Red hyphens.

A hunter fires in the wood.
A movement behind the leaves ceases.

If I think of all those
elder poems I tried to write
--even those that some have liked--
they lie at my feet
like leaves that once nourished
the growing maple by the
kitchen door,
                    and I would
rather look at the tree itself,
wondering,
                    what leaves this year?
I said lie?
                    Yes, they lie there,
but not all lies.

                              My own Naiad
Features of any time.
Let's take the afternoon.

Why, *yes*, all sex and curves
that walk through what I see
and may not be.

I have become involved in serial composition. ... But that is only one part of the work--only that material which dictates such a procedure. So it is all a voicing.

                              --T. E. 6/4/87

TRANCE

1

Tenth

                              seraphic distance
grey, along the gardenpath sky, echoing speed in a tucked
thought under my hand (a flame by coincidence of the
eye). At night, reversing their zones, what small shadows
of blue they fan.

Scallion chunk fastener in Europe below the bevel taking
tea in unbecoming style. He's wearing a Thursday suit.
The other speaking music from fatigue

                              where for your
pleasure each tone coincides, coils, fades: a lucid
slope of trees angled in a trace or the river she did
stand beside.

             The past irrevocably narrows into a garden.
My finger, poised

               above these failing lights, with ellipse,
with hoverings-down and roof-tales to sway

                          poniards,
like a pensionary's fool.

2

Ordinary eyes of paraffin (the garden pentangle, The Land
of Beulah)

Thinned ardors fleck the path. She frets the veneer (inlaid
with quickness). Elastic swerve. The wing of an insect. The
aerial motives of her speech (inside the ridge parting the
seam) extend the margins of its home. Low channels in the
northern sphere, streakbeds, her voice resounding them all

any flower?

                                                like that of horn

(suggesting sugar cane) reciprocal daze. The treasure-rail
positions the train, escorts with a generous motion imitating
silence.

3

She stood back, viewing him tautly, her eyebrows steadied
and immovable

                             drift, drift

below the silent town, the dwelling-wind bridge. I was
alone, finding time.

                         An unexpected (forgive me). See
how those animations in the clerestory, unfixed from
their angles, distort in the act of being heard
& silence themselves in descent

                                     (looking
glass)

      reasoned by clairvoyance, the privilege of the
silver head of a man. His authority reflects the
apparent position in which he falsely appears: but only
half of him (ringed with flowers)--

                         the other half escapes
& is envied.

4

Tell me your name for dreariness. Tell me I didn't know what
to say

              ocellus peeps on a peacock frame.

Step back when the sky obscures & the rains fall in a famous
novel. Treasures of incondensable fog surround your throat.
Delicacy of perceptions left in the room. The salt missing
from the table. The drinks grown cold.

                        what absurdity
sleeps
here

                Oceania, a neglected sky.

Iron of knowledge. The heavy stand held by a rope under the
high vault to prevent the rush of respectable acts opposite
me.   There's a thin hand divides us, the merest shadow.
Its transparency quickens you. I buy your words in ascending
shapes: gutters, spheres, sinks, impedimenta. I accompany
their surfaces.

5

Mahogany narrows. They walk upon the same inches,
disconcertingly alive. Many streams flow there.
She exhibits something like violence. The confrontatory
sound of the train. Take it one step.Documents
escape

      the flatness of certain dreams. I am awake:
any flowers? The spoon is hope. The shallownesses.
Whisper-room, hush extravagance! An accurate
perception begins to weaken. Five women sit in the
shadow of the watertank.

      Milkmaids watching a star.
The implications of the scone. Taciturn weather.
She repeats the sounds, but the tiny differences...
Ask the Nazirite. Faintly, in the night sky.

6

The year these old writings unravelled and fell on those
who loved their life at the high wood traced from the
sun & stood at stake by the pail beside the box, their
truth withered, waded through wasting breath, far back,
where they could not tell. Aboveboard, mentioned for
forty days on three roads at once, led four men to
the dell. Lean your eye into the word of spells double-
fold as it takes its way. A girl's name

                          of a thickness
underneath the ox-hide where it draws. (After three
hours I returned home with hesitation. But I was not
made to feel guilty, or disgraced, or prodigal; everyone
seemed friendly & appreciative, as though I had done
them some great service.) The palace was originally
a fence, then the dwellers came. How many sounds emerged
from the pool.

           I saw them by the rooftop fountain.
I heard a noise like the tip of a fly.

Levels of Address

Why start with a self-reflexive question? The imperative levels address. What I have needed, simply to get off, is that illusion of form address implies. The bi- or multi- polar, talking to.

One hour from now is waiting. What anxiety inheres, wants out, to bud. So much behavior, between us, fixes our suspicions. But I have tools to make an index.

I am satisfied with very little. Dusk begins my day and continues in lengths, undifferentiated. Write neither of, nor substitute, to keep you, reading. After all, honesty is only custom, or better, custom is custom. Each full page waits against argument, then, taken from neglects, asks questions.

Watch what falls from this tree. Step up and shake. Name's__________. Was that mine? Come closer.

Observe, speak. Inequivalent in method, but essentially questions. Always letting one out, then sorting fish. What is the gesture for breadth of acceptance? Once you start interpreting things, it's hard to stop, and who's to say you should? A man arrives with a big white sheet; the ice gets thicker. Think of you think of yourself.

What current language is available to us all, a gloss and pitch, more than its freight determines commonality.

How many are you? I write a letter to the one I love best. Some write back, but never really does. Love wasn't the idea.

Finding the time for many receipt, as, consolidating many to one, times, harden. That is difficult. Compose, be calm. Theft takes a steady hand, and patience. How many are you, hear me?

Never minding what's said, is intransitive implies you. Take my advice. Questions, toasts, confessions, suggestions...lead. To me. Look at it from my point of view. From consensus hums like a house, or other pleasant-sounding logic, always plain. Get by the neck and think it.

Remember my days in what slow fluid. I anticipate yours, suggest a beat. Look at yourself. I'll bet you're attracted to music, to beautiful fabrics. An agreement we rewrite. My currency in yours, grace.

We are concerned
each
with you on your flight
art accustomed to one moment
only me. That you have committed
act independently,
redundantly to yourself.

Strength
a prayer work fecundate
alone, a footprint, two
won't hear. We send
slip into an envelope conceived
outside our text's
necessary reference.

Lord, speak
futurity. These difficult
in our hands fragments value
that you will commit to raise
child, precursor.
Small faith
take.

He'd left her a note, tomorrow.

Chance precedes a shudder, which pops on before dawn. Venus,
weak by comparison, is drowned in the difficulty. Light in his eyes,
blinding him, hubby piled up his rig, tied up the
highway. Past harbors, harbors examples. Without means, the
shudder keeps running. She snaps the lead.

"The problem with him
insistence, with no need to answer any questions. Person
unnecessary, address diffuse. I can report to you that he.
Started in mid-step, he ran. We might erect a fence, or just
suggest limits, arbiter. Either way without a doubt.

You'd by what I call necessity, by what's inherent. I want
to go back from the light in my eyes. I might make it a
narrative's already done. The project

Figures of Production

Who's listening? There's nothing to look at, fix your eyes. There's time to
reconfigure what you might see. Be careful.

A characteristic gesture, a tic has soiled utility. Pare off what's intended to
the true routine. In this scene shank rests left right left right an
idiosyncratic sway to the pelvis like grinding his teeth. What sounds
destined's but the next corner, arriving tired.

Figures of production. The terms mean less when used. Listen to the facts
pulling a needle through my cloth. Too often short of breath. Fact
complecting needle's skill puts to run, a daily threat. Rules to live by

> observing any given
> through

But I'll embellish what I see, seeing in fact sentiment.

> resistance, not as stone, but stone
> better left

At the instant of discrimination, at the seed of the rationale, fist over hand.
Who holds out his hand? Who's paying? Payment is artifice. Their linkage is
linguistic, poverty as well of the same equation. Agreement or violence.

> Knowing what a knife cut
> too keep the place clean

Don't rest. Don't describe. You won't fail to be burned. Like.

> to empty
> my life

> cautious to the last atom
> nesia's implied to stay alive

Debunking spiritual poverty as a thing not yet successfully defined, sup with
us. Do you know where your next meal is coming from? I saw a very nice
one in a window downtown. Who'll say grace?

My can't help comparing mine to theirs. I continue shrinking. I am taller by
far. Do you like the way I strut and spit?

congruence and plentitude

remember who I am at any moment. Resisting returning. On a shelf in the
second of those rooms, something I've made rests. Paper and clay
uncertainly. Now I want to test the man on the phone, at the counter, my
desk. You and I listening hear the similarity. Multiply.

the determinant
act preceding insight, from that dark gradually
your face, and then, as if into myself

repeatedly and without distinction

Talking about
the violence in the act, how plain expression accumulates a code. I want to
touch and you, to be absent. The pauses, countenance, become perfect alum.
The pauses

privileged to talk about loving you. The rest of the language is out on strike.
Who will replace the woman never correctly thought? The question is wrong,
but one of intention. At what point has she retreated?

       Strange to judge a man, dancing with him. Too loud to talk
keeps them from me. We need this formality for practice, simulating in the
mood. I like to keep my thoughts short.
       I asked him when the machine would be free, the whole day
so a month or year, a coin in my mouth. He's at the controls, profile, full
view, identifiable. I hate the model to the real thing, who's just turned away
again.

sex of the air, my
hips
mind behavior alone among books
fine
to achieve notoriety
set
that tree to the rectangular
heat

pays on receipt
keeps his thoughts to himself. Remember the guy in the red suit?
Downpayment is a disease like any other. A habit. Keep your eyes on street
level, off folk, there's goods

occupy affection. So shoot me. There's no law says I can't

impersonate

fellow professionals. Pornography in the age of mechanical reproduction. Reproduction itself. Hip to axle, spoke of water rising to a well. The skin like a rubber tarp, pulled over it, wave register.

When
symmetry in two lines
and a gap between

enough
past into myself waiting
for him at the door

omit my black
skirt, the look she never

business
done in there.

Visual Voice 21

Homophonic Explosions in Two Poems Collapsing into One
As it Drifts Through an Alphabetic Minefield

Wyatt, "Hate whom ye list," from <u>Additional Ms. 17492</u>
Barnabe Googe, "To Doctor Bale"

The two poems, originally unlike, accidentally meet and interconnect lines, becoming a monster of a single poem as it drifts through an alphabetic minefield. The lettristic mines explode as any homophone in the new poem's lines moves past a horizontal potency point.

Hate whom ye list, fo I ca e not,
Good aged Bale, that with thy hoary hair
 ove whom ye lis and spare no ,
Dost yet persist to t rn the painf l book,
Do what ye list and dread not,
   happy man, that hast obtained such years,
Think what ye list, I fear not,
And leav'st not et on papers pale to look,
For, as for me, I am not
Give over now to be t thy we ried br in,
But even as one that recks not
And rest thy pen that long hath labored sore;
Whether ye hate or hate not;
For ag d m n unfit sur is such pain,
For in your love I dote not,
And thee beseems to labor now no more.
W erefore I pray you forget not,
But thou, I th nk, Don Plato's part w ll play,
 ut love whom ye list, for I care not.
With boo in hand to have thy dying day.

Visual Voice 47

Poem as Mental Convergence Towards Its Two Finest Lines

William Alabaster

Upon The Crucifix

Now I have found thee I will evermore
Embrace this standard where thou sitts above,
Feede greedie eies, and from hence never rove;
Sucke hungrie soule of this eternall store;
Issue my hart from thie two leaved dore,
And lett my lippes from kissinge not remove.
O that I weare transformed into love,
And as a plant might springe uppon this flower,
Like wandring Ivy or sweet honnie suckle:
How would I with my twine about it buckle,
And kisse his feete with my ambitious boughes,
And clyme along uppon his sacred brest,
And make a garland for his wounded browes:
Lord soe I am, if heare my thoughts may rest.

with my twine about it buckle.
his feete with my ambitious boughs,
I with my twine about it buckle,
his feete with my ambitious boughs,
ld I with my twine about it buckle,
se his feete with my ambitious boughs,
ould I with my twine about it buckle,
isse his feete with my ambitious boughs,
would I with my twine about it buckle,
kisse his feete with my ambitious boughs,
ow would I with my twine about it buckl,e
nd kisse his feete with my ambitious boughs,
    How would I with my twine about it buckle,
    And kisse his feete with my ambitious boughs,
     How would I with my twine about it buckle,
     And kisse his feete with my ambitious boughs,
      How would I with my twine about it buckle,
      And kisse his feete with my ambitious boughs,
       How would I with my twine about it buckle,
       And kisse his feete with my ambitious boughs,
        How would I with my twine about it buckle,
        And kisse his feete with my ambitious boughs,
         How would I with my twine about it buckle,
         And kisse his feete with my ambitious boughs,
          How would I with my twine about it buckle,
          And kisse Now I have found thee I will evermore
           How wou Embrace this standard where thou sitts above,
           And kis Feede greedie eies, and from hence never rove;
            How w Sucke hungrie soule of this eternall store;
            And k Issue my hart from thie two leaved dore,
             How And lett my lippes from kissinge not remove.
             And O that I weare tranformed into love,
              H And as a plant might springe uppon this flower,
              A Like wandering Ivy or seete honnie suckle:
                How would I with my twine about it buckle,
                And kisse his feete with my ambitious boughes,
              H And clyme along uppon his sacred brest,
              A And make a garland for his wounded browes:
             How Lord soe I am, if heare my thoughts may rest.
             And kisse his feete with my ambitious boughs,
            How would I with my twine about it buckle,
            And kisse his feete with my ambitious boughs,
           How would I with my twine about it buckle,
           And kisse his feete with my ambitious boughs,
          How would I with my twine about it buckle,
          And kisse his feete with my ambitious boughs,
         How would I with my twine about it buckle,
         And kisse his feete with my ambitious boughs,
        How would I with my twine about it buckle,
        And kisse his feete with my ambitious boughs,
       How would I with my twine about it buckle,
       And kisse his feete with my ambitious boughs,
      How would I with my twine about it buckle,
      And kisse his feete with my ambitious boughs,
     How would I with my twine about it buckle,
     And kisse his feete with my ambitious boughs,
    How would I with my twine about it buckle,
    And kisse his feete with my ambitious boughs,
How would I with my twine about it buckle,
And kisse his feete with my ambitious boughs,
w would I with my twine about it buckle,
d kisse his feete with my ambitious boughs,
would I with my twine about it buckle,

Her window, small, cracked: its emptiness
magnifies the room --she's huge
face to face with blurred mob scenes

--her table is immense, train stations
ball parks --all those clippings, covered
as when a great statue still veiled
feels its blood beginning to move :a fold
that wasn't there before

--she will smoothe the bulge, over and over
accuse the papers, magazines, their pictures
for years waiting motionless
and under her table cloth

--she will look only at crowds
--he couldn't get out if he wanted
even if that's him with the hat
or no hat and where is this place

this under the ground where everyone
is always gathered, waiting
for the gentle handhold, the first sound

the weeping for strangers --she will swell
enormous over the moonlight
over his stillness and the way.

from THE POETICS OF COMMON KNOWLEDGE

> *Poiesis is the work of fabricating a formal intelligibility out of...disparate and logically irreconcilable factors of existence. To accomplish this means to develop a heightened sense of proportion and scale, to negotiate a feeling for the apt and the inapt in the total corporeal aptitude with which one addresses the world.*
>
> --Jed Rasula

1) Autopoiesis

The phenomenologists' program, *to return to things in themselves*, appears to lead almost immediately back to things other than themselves. This truth is now widely taken as axiomatic. Derrida: "...contrary to what phenomenology--which is always phenomenology of perception--has tried to make us believe, contrary to what our desire cannot fail to be tempted into believing, the thing itself always escapes."

The reason Derrida's argument has seemed so important, especially to American readers, is not clear. To the pioneers of American phenomenology, William James and C.S. Peirce, it was obviously, a controlling factor in the development of pragmatism. Derrida's proposition is moreover a tautology, albeit a somewhat sneaky one: the parenthetical qualification of phenomenology as "phenomenology of perception" emphasizes an implicit encoding, and the escape of the thing itself into the perceptual code is a submerged logical necessary. The closed proposition, however, is freighted with dissonant emotional content. Its logic is overlaid with an implicit narrative of desire, pursuit, and failure. The eros that deploys its own sufficiency as its identity excludes the very thing that it desires. For Derrida, the thing itself, the perfect logical thing which justifies the thought, is consigned to an alien domain even before thought begins. Phenomenology is both contrasted to logic and defined in terms of it; the infinite recursion is implicit

in the definition itself. As a cultural strategy, it seems almost too foolish to take seriously, but its centrality to western thought cannot be denied, and, while Derrida does not defend it, he cannot find an articulate alternative, only the Nietzschean laughter and dance.

Nothing in language or in community, however, requires the existence of perfectly logical things, and, as Wittgenstein has shown, it is hard to say what use our belief in them actually serves. This point is made by one of his most famous examples:

Suppose everyone had a box with something in it: we call it a "beetle". No one can look into anyone else's box, and everyone says he knows what a beetle is only by looking at "his" beetle. --Here it would be quite possible for everyone to have something different in his box. One might even imagine such a thing constantly changing.

The beetle is a creature of the myth which obligated us to our symbolism. As long as mind was confined to limited abstraction--that is, as long as it was mind as such, suspended between incommensurables, between abstract systematicity and a substantial world--the status of symbolism could not be clarified. A fact was at once an object of contemplation and an assertion of purpose, even an act of domination, which involved a mythical self and a mythical world, including mythical beetles, birds, physical forces, atoms, societies, social forces, and so forth. The Greeks were able to conceive of pure abstraction, of thought thinking itself but only in this century have we learned the practical procedures of such thought. We have learned to think not only of abstract systems but also of the systematicity of abstract systems. For us, the content of abstraction is not substance but systematicity itself.

The western philosophic project left us unprepared for this success: we devoted ourselves to developing the ultimate wrench without developing the ultimate nut and bolt. Thus, we have great leverage but nothing on which to get a purchase. We are left peculiarly worldless. To be sure, it is possible to describe a world or, more accurately, an endless succession of possible worlds, each providing a rational frame of reference. We do not know, however, which of these worlds we inhabit. As both observers of the world and critics of our own observational practice, we must see that the choice of a frame of reference is fraught with paradox: the choice can only be made from within some frame which prejudices the decision. For over two millennia we have pursued the perfectly logical object, and we are now in danger of submitting to a rationality which does not even have the dignity of beginning and end.

Luckily, the systematicity of the social machine as information processor is not ideal--indeed its architecture is necessarily open: it cannot, therefore, assert total, rational control of society. Contemporary systemic thought is, however, more than powerful enough to control any *particular* domain. It can constitute an effectively absolute system from relativistic subsystems. In this connection, Donna Haraway writes of the regime of the "Informatics of Domination":

One should expect control strategies to concentrate on boundary conditions, on rates of flow across boundaries--and not on the integrity of natural objects... Human beings, like any other component or subsystem, must be localized in a system architecture whose basic modes of operation are probabilistic, statistical. No objects, space, or bodies are sacred in themselves; any component can be interfaced with any other if the proper standard, the proper code, can be constructed for processing signals in a common language.

The assimilation of human behavior to the theoretical requirements of abstract description results in the profound alienation that distinguishes a culture devoted to producing information rather than material goods. Under the regime of the informatics of domination, values are determined not by the assertion of an holistic ideal but by the making of distinctions. Wherever a distinction is made, a world comes into existence, local values are instituted, and controls can be established. The clearest expositions of these techniques that I know are to be found in Stafford Beer's remarkable studies of the theory of management. As he elegantly demonstrates, systems are not constituted of matter and motion, as the Newtonian model assumed, but of information and purpose, and they are sustained not by the input of energy (i.e. a kinetic form of matter) but by the input of information. Everything is relative *and* everything is implicitly controllable.

Control is implicitly exercised not from the perspective of totality but from the perspective which is *immediately* superior to the instituting distinction. Of course, any agent of control may be in turn controlled from a superior perspective, but--and this is the surprising fact--the logic of the various perspectives need not be consistent. Consider the complex system in Figure 1 [Next page]. It consists of four subsystems which are subordinate to the purpose of AAA. It is eros, not logic, which establishes closed systems, and as long as AAA satisfies its purpose, the system remains closed or conversely as long as the system remains closed, the purpose of AAA is satisfied. As the figure shows, a local control network accepts input from unresolved totality (i.e. language, writing, information) and ultimately returns its output to the same paradoxical domain. Inside the closed system, however, purpose is served by the reduction of variety; unresolved totality is locally resolved.

In our illustration, the A's, B's, and C's might be anything. And realistically, the diagram would be criss-crossed with other systems, showing that the individuals participate in a vast ordering network. Powerful control mechanisms are possible, and their laws are known: control is in effect

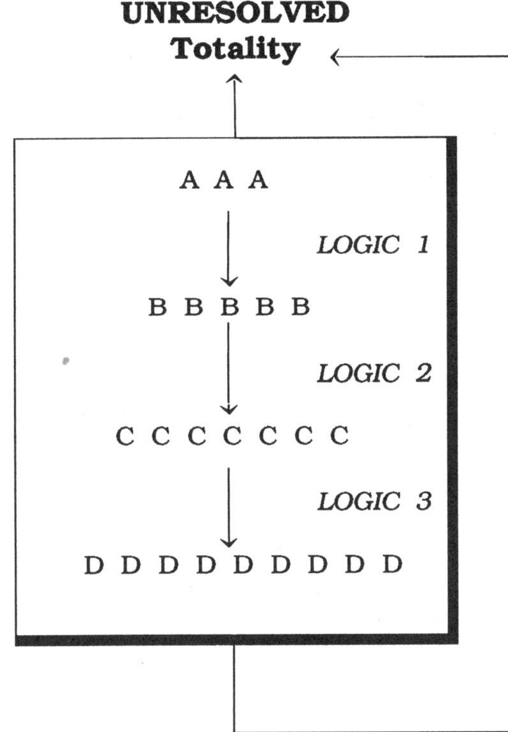

control.

There may be only one distinction which does not exhibit this symmetry. Humberto Maturana writes:

The observer beholds simultaneously the entity that he considers (an organism, in our case) and the universe in which it lies (the organism's environment). This allows him to interact independently with both and to have interactions that are necessarily outside the domain of interactions of the observed entity.

The boundary of the domain of the observed entity is unique: its inside can be descibed but its outside cannot be; therefore, the observer cannot be subsumed by defining a more general domain. Individuals themselves cannot be described, only their relationships. It is thus possible to distinguish between the "organization" of an organism and the "structure" of an organism. Its organization consists of its self-producing identity, for which all describable structures are merely contingent means. Its structure consists of the describable relationships which it establishes with its domain of interactions.

The autopoetic machine, as Maturana and Varela call the living organism, therefore, has a dual character: it is at once self-producing and responsible only to its own unique identity and it is also a mechanism that functions in the processes of evolution, history, geneology, and so forth.

An autopoietic machine is a machine organized (defined as a unity) as a network of processes of production (transformation and destruction) of components that produces the components which: (i) through their interactions and transformations continuously regenerate and realize the network of processes (relations) that produce them; and (ii) constitute it (the machine) as a concrete unity in the space in which they (the components) exist by specifying the topological domain of its realization as such as network.

This account is sufficient as a theoretical grounds for the scientific project: it establishes the possibility of integrity for scientific observers and a describable real-

a reduction of variety. At each level of subordination, there is a proliferation of sameness: the logic of BBBB produces the uniformity of CCCCC and so forth. The regime, however, is not totalitarian--that is, it does not invoke a totality or absolute. The principle of control, as we learn from cybernetics, is itself paradoxical: *only variety reduces variety.* AAA (which, incidentally, is not itself a unified principle) creates control in its domain by generating variety--that is, by creating conditions under which the sub-systems can each satisfy their own purposes. Therefore, it is not only not necessary even that the three logics be consistent. Indeed, so long as they can be isolated from one another, the order of the system as a whole is potentially increased by their inconsistency. Of course, this gain in order is not free. Just as an internal combustion engine requires an input of fuel, a cybernetic machine requires the input of information. When common distinctions are made, structures which are the expressions of purpose appear. They need only be fed information from the domain of resolved totality to begin to establish

ity, which of course may include the "observer," as in contemporary physics. The observers are observed in relationship to the observed world but not in relation to themselves as self-referring and self-producing entities. It is however the organization of the observing organisms not their structures which are served. Maturana and Varela:

Thus, the individuals, though transitory, are essential, not dispensable, because they constitute a necessary condition for the existence of the historical network which they define. The species is only an abstract entity in the present, and although it represents a historical phenomenon it does not constitute a generative factor in the phenomenology of evolution, it is the result.

This statement provides the grounds for an alternative to the informatics of domination. Although individuals constitute communicating networks, they are not subsumed by the conditions of observation. Individuals are not the creatures of their observation or subject to the logic of their descriptions. As Maturana and Varela note, the DNA code no more carries the information that specifies an individual organism than a political constitution carries the information that specifies the history of a country (DNA code, as Wittgenstein says of all concepts, is not for use on single occasions).

Maturana and Varela account only for a silent domain of phenomena, which can be absorbed in wordless meditation, and a domain of description. The poetics of common knowledge is concerned neither with the *being* of the individual as a substratum of descriptive, scientific discourse nor with description itself but a measure of value. Therefore, it insists upon a linguistic dualism, upon a fundamental incompatibility in the linguistic field. It does not continue the familiar dualisms of mind-body, subject-object, culture-nature, man-woman, good-evil, and so forth; these are all slippery distinctions, without certain boundaries, and they belong to the domain of description, which is to say the domain of disciplined knowledge, statistical reality, and systemic domination. If language is understood as an uninterpreted calculus and meaning as an interpretation of it, as it is by most of the schools of linguistic philosophy, every distinction is inevitably fluid. If however the logic and meaning of language are both given together in their use, it is possible to look and see what is meant. Integrity will depend upon the degree of concrete specification in the situation, not upon its theoretical coherence.

A concrete life remains to be constructed. We cannot wait for the ideological matters to be settled, because, of course, settlement is not in the nature of institutional life. Without a domain of common knowledge in terms of which institutional life can be interpreted, however, the unsettlement will not be generative, as it might be, but muddled, desperate, and absurd, guided, as it has been in this century, by nothing more than the hope to produce an efficient mechanism which can be substituted for our lives.

2) The Continuum: The Place of Poetry

Autopoiesis does not establish the conditions for the publication and thus commonality of poetry, which of course requires language. Maturana and Varela introduce two domains, only one of which is linguistic: the domain of the self-producing and self-identical organism and the domain of description: in one, A stands for itself and only itself, and, in the other, B stands for A. This B is B not because of its self-identity but because of its systematic relations to other entities which constitute the medium and which must be maintained as a discipline, a task which in our culture is increasingly consigned to professionals. The domain of the common, which was once the burden of folk culture, the active and creative functions of life, as opposed to the merely descriptive and regulatory, must now be specifically constituted. Charles Olson's redaction of Hesiodic cosmology addresses this necessity directly:

The sea was born of the earth without sweet union of love Hesiod says

*But that then she lay for heaven and she
bare the things which encloses every thing,
Okeanos the one which all things are and
by which nothing is anything but itself,
measured so*

*screwing earth, in whom love lies which
unnerves the limbs and by its heat floods
the mind and all gods and men into further
nature.*

Okeanos is the principle of autopoiesis.
The distance from Maturana's and Varela's
"described so" to Olson's "measure so" is
the distance from the domain of the mech-
anistic and statistical to the domain of the
creative and active. In the domain of
description, nature is fixed as a realm of
possible worlds; in the domain of the
creative, the heat of love "floods the
mind...into *further* nature," which is the
realization of the contingent facticity of the
organism.

Language as description is well under-
stood; the science of linguistics has been
devoted to it almost exclusively. As a con-
crete act of measure which relates us to a
manifest concreteness, however, the poem
potentially gives us extraordinary access to
our own participation in the construction of
the world. William Carlos Williams:

*How shall we get said what must be said?
Only the poem.*

*Only the counted poem, to an exact
    measure:*
    . . .

*Only the made poem, the verb calls it
                into being.*

The poem "counted" and "made" calls "it"
into being. In this case *it* is a form--
abstract, unreal, a description--which may
be a man or a woman, asleep or dead, on
the bridge between Juarez and El Paso,
and with it, called also into being, a dance
and a music. by the end of the poem,
Williams calls out:

*I am a poet! I
am. I am. I am a poet, I reaffirmed,
                    ashamed*

*Now the music volleys through as in a
lonely moment I hear it. Now it is all
about me. The dance! The verb detaches
                    itself*

seeking to become articulate.

The name of being a poet is great: the
concreteness of who and what one is is
thoroughly exposed. Williams cannot avoid
ending the poem with a nod to conventional
romanticism, but the verb detaching itself
and seeking the articulation of concrete
motion in itself cannot be comfortably
assimilated. To bring a dynamic world into
view by peformance is to expose the static
symbolism which draws international
boundaries and makes other logical
distinction by way of symbolic proliferation,
whether in international politics, mathe-
matics, or elsewhere.

I derive the distinction on which my
argument is poised from Henri Poincaré's
Science and Hypothesis, a book which had
a significant impact on Henry Adams, the
Cubist painters, Marcel Duchamp, and thus
on subsequent twentieth-century art. The
distinction was not original with Poincaré,
but his particular terms which were local to
a critical moment of cultural mutation are
appropriate. He gives us a most general
statement of the insight which gave rise in
this century to art which proposes not to
describe but to enact or, as Williams says,
to dance. In an economical enactment of
that dance, Robert Creeley writes:

    *--it
     it--* (CP, 391).

In effect, the distinction to be made is
between "it" and "it" measured through
three beats of time, counting the silent beat
which separates them.

Nothing is simpler or more fundamental
than counting. When we say that something
is a simple as one-two-three, we mean that
is *also* as simple as four-five-six. The
continuum, to put matters on precisely the
tautological level we require, continues.
Poincaré takes an example from an
important experiment of Gustav Theodor
Fechner, one of the founders of experi-
mental psychology. It was crucial to the

development of statistical methods in the social sciences, and through the work of C.S. Peirce, who replicated it and improved the methodology, and the work of Poincaré, it had important philosophic consequences. Poincaré develops the example in these terms: the physical continuum is established by an experiment which asks the subject to distinguish objects by the sensation of their weights and arrange them in ascending order of heaviness. In this situation,

It has been observed that a weight of 10 grammes and a weight of 11 grammes produced identical sensations, that the weight B could no longer be distinguished from a weight C of 12 grammes, but that the weight A was readily distinguished from the weight C. Thus the rough results of the experiment may be expressed by the following relations: A=B, B=C, A<C, which may be regarded as the formula of the physical continuum. But here is an intolerable disagreement with the law of contradiction...

At first the paradox seems so simple as to be more than a trick, but careful examination will indicate that the problem appears in any attempt to represent a sensation. Phenomenal intuition and the representation of intuition have different requirements. Clearly the problem cannot be solved by a more accurate measuring device; it is inherent in the nature of measurement as such. More accurate measurement makes the terms of the paradox subtler, but, at some point, the ability to discriminate breaks down. Even the most sensitive chemical balance finally cannot distinguish between quantities. The physical continuum does not obey the law of transivity: A=B, B=C, therefore, A=C. It is not a trivial matter: the loss of this law is tantamount to affirming 0=1. Curiously, the experience of the atomic nature of measured space confirms the continuity of sensation. If A and B cannot be physically distinguished from one another, A and C must be distinguished as a function of the act of measurement itself, not inherent in the nature of space.

Poincaré notes that the conception of space and thus of continuity arises specifically from muscular or proprioceptive experience: "Not only could this concept not be derived from a single sensation, or even from a series of sensations; but a motionless being could never have acquired it, because, not being able to correct by his movements the effects of the change of position of external objects, he would have had no reason to distinguish them from changes of state." Space and our knowledge of its continuity are not separable from our movement in it. If we did not move and establish a space measured by the discrete units of the motion, nothing would be separated from anything else. Indeed we can only conclude that the phenomena of spatiality are results of a specific human scale. When we inquire into the spatial nature of either cosmic or sub-atomic events, the evidence seems to support quite different structures. The categories of experience are required not by logic but by the concrete nature of experience itself. John Cage:

The daily warmth
experience, my father said, is not
transmitted by Sun to Earth but is what
Earth does in response to Sun.
Measurements, he said, measure
measuring means.

In order to avoid the logical problem, it is necessary to define a continuum on which there is always a point between any two points, though it may involve units so small they cannot be measured; that is, it is necessary to move from phenomena to phenome*logy*. As Poincaré notes, this solution involves the construction of "the symbolic continuum, which is only a particular system of symbols." That is, it is possible to make a symbol for which there is no corresponding intuition.

In the practical terms of Fechner's experiment, this means that the trials were tallied as either heavier or lighter, instances of indecision being evenly distributed between the categories. This procedure sparked a lively debate in statistical analysis during the last two decades of the Nineteenth Century and after. Stephen M. Stigler summarizes the alternatives which were considered in his excellent *The History of Statistics: The Measurement of Uncertainty before 1900*:

1) Follow Fechner's approach an divide the doubtful cases between right and wrong.

2) Calculate two values of h *[Fechner's term for individual sensitivity] and average them: one with all doubtful cases treated as right, and one with all treated as wrong...*

3) Insist that no doubtful answers be allowed, so that all answer became right or wrong.

One way or another, all of these methods eliminate undecidable cases. It seems a trivial matter perhaps, but it is in the practical detail of experimental procedures that abstraction and purpose enter, and in hundreds of similar "practical" situations where we are required to observe the "reality" of symbolic entities that our participation in the world of disciplined knowledge is lost. Our experience is seldom of a tyrannical experimenter, saying "*Choose!* You *must* decide!" but a friendly, smiling person, saying, "Well, what do you think?" or even more frequently, it is ourselves, in a quandary, and taking this or that chance. One by one, none of the decisions is important. If, however, no decision is important individually, how do collections of such decisions attain importance? The subject's obligation is transferred from the experience to the symbolism.

The symbolic continuum consists not of an enumerable extension but of discrete relationships. It is without scale: there are an infinite number of intangible points between any two points. Having once made a commitment to this no-space, it is impossible to stop making distinctions and defining new points. In the attempt to make sense of the first symbol--to read it--we make more symbols, regressing infinitely into the space of the Zenonian paradoxes, where the rabbit never catches the tortoise, the arrow, which at every infinitely small moment of time is at rest, never reaches the target, and so forth. Symbolism defines a *static* world. Things cannot move from one point to another because every point is discrete.

Far from being a simple trick, the paradox is decisive for Hegelian phenomenology, for example. Sense certainty is judged to be inferior to language precisely because it proves to be logically intransitive. Hegel gives this account of the physical time continuum:

The Now is pointed to, this Now; it has already ceased to be in the act of pointing to it [i.e. A=B]. The Now that is is another Now than the one pointed to, and we see that the Now is just this: to be no more just when it is [B=C]. The Now, as it is pointed out to us, is Now that has been, and this is its truth; it has not the truth of being [A=C]. Yet this much is true, that it has been.

This character of reality is, Hegel says, "unutterable...the untrue, the irrational." The attempt to express it unsays itself, revealing the contradiction which justifies the substitution of the symbolic for the physical continuum. For Hegel, this unsaying constitutes the languages's guarantee for itself; it is thus like the *Pentateuch*, telling the story which establishes its own authority. Carrying Cartesian methodology a step further, Hegel substitutes linguistic logic for algebraic logic and words for rigorously defined alphabetic signs, an essential development in the pre-history of the logical calculus and contemporary information-handling technology, despite the inherent lack of rigor. History is understood not as the product of the temporal continuum but as the narrative of the attempt to rationalize accumulated symbolism in its relation to the past and future, which are at once open to inspection and symbolically infinite.

There are thus two modes of intuition. In the concrete mode of intuition, *each thing is itself and exists only through itself.* In the other mode, the subject, which is a center of purposive behavior, divides the intuitive epistemic domain into a class of tokens and a class of objects, and notes relationships: *each thing is related to and has meaning through some other thing.* It is algebraic or functional intuition, and its product is description. These two domains of knowledge, the knowledge of individuals, which we have by virtue of our own radical independence as living beings, and the knowledge of relationships, are thrown together in the person, by cosmic chance for all we know. There seems at least to be no necessary connection between them.

The poet proposes to engage language as measure without capitulating to its logic. Thus, poetry takes up language in its temporal and physical characters; it is concerned as much with dynamism as with form, as much with breath and vibrations in air as with distinctive, phonemic features, as much with typography as reference, as much with embodiment of trope as with meaning of trope.

In his masterful study of African drumming, John Miller Chernoff makes a useful distinction between "rhythm as something to 'get with'" and "rhythm...as something to 'respond to.'" "In African music," he writes, "it is the listener or dancer who has to supply the beat: the music itself does not become the concentrated focus of an event."Rhythm is directionless and purposeless, a medium of indeterminate topology, which is created moment by moment and step by step. Rhythm is the physical continuum of Poincaré, and its flow is characterized by the paradox, A=B, B=C, C<A--that is, instant A cannot be distinguished from instant B but instant C can be distinguished from A. Time in this sense is shapeless and directionless.

In poetry, the measure is taken not merely in terms of a beat but of the complex activity of a human organism speaking. We do not measure with a cadence alone, though such has been a common practice since the appearance of abstract poetic forms. In poetry, *language* is the measure of rhythm. Measure is compelling only to those who participate in its performance and for whom it is utterly obvious. We agree, to the extent that we do, because we are roughly the same kinds of beings, or so we infer by virtue of the interest we take in one another's linguistic productions. Otherwise our attempts to come into contact inevitably takes the form of compulsion, and so, the medium is exaggerated at the expense of every one who attempts to use it. The inflation of the medium is responsible for the current intellectual impoverishment.

This, I understand, is to reintroduce chaos where we appeared to have escaped it. As Wittgenstein writes, however, "Everyday language is a part of the human organism and is no less complicated than it." A heart beats; a chest muscle contracts; a mouth eats, kisses, and speaks. The mouth speaking, the hand writing, furthermore, are precisely the acts which carry the organism beyond homeostasis. If the purpose of common speech is to reveal a piece of information or the form of a thought, it does not do so apart from revealing its associations with the organism as a whole, and when it reaches by way of language out beyond the automatic controls which return the organism to equilibrium the dangers are grave. They are also inevitable: consciousness is the desperation of the cosmos to know itself.

Poetic sequences exist only in the self-obstructive environments of the language which makes them manifest. They must contend with the multiple demands of a speaking body and its limitations, the cussedness of physical world, and the silence of the interior sense. The inherent dynamism of rhythm is tense and often deflected. Robert Creeley:

I keep to myself such
measures as I care for,
daily the rocks
accumulate position.

There is nothing
but what thinking makes
it less tangible. The mind
fast as it goes, loses

pace, puts in place of it
like rocks simple markers
for a way only to
hopefully come back to

where it cannot. All
forgets. My mind sinks.
I hold in both hands such weight
it is my only description.

(Words)

Measurement is a self-obstructing activity;

the dimensions get in one another's way, and, if space and time are conceived as rigid, they must be despised and subverted. We have consistently sought to exhibit meaning, to stage it in a representational medium, where there is access to motion. Our exhibited image, however, requires a more and more elaborate theatrical setting, and we have begun to reach a point of diminishing returns.

Measured time is rhythm in relation to human action and, therefore, human scale. It is also purposeless. It does not search for infinitesimals, but it knows none; it does not undertake the reconciliation of the one and the many, for it is poised on the experience of a physical continuum on which already--unproblematically--0=1 and 1=2. The measure is not a count of so many pre-existent beats or so many pre-existent steps. The track from 0 to 1 and from 1 to 2 is *not* along a pre-existent road but comes into existence only with the song and dance. Zeno's paradoxes are logically irrefutable; they are overcome not by argument but by movement.

MANIFESTO OF
THE COMMON KNOWLEDGE

The first act of the poetics of common knowledge is to dissociate poetry from poetic language, in particular from those aspects of language which invite comparison to organisms or to computer software, but also the languages of magic, shamanism, esoterism, and the carnival, to recall the Kristeva's sources of poetic language; fundamentally poetry has to do neither with the rationalization of language nor with its subversion. It seems odd to say that poetry is not linguistic, at least in one of its most significant moments, but such seems to be the case. Robert Duncan:

I want to describe Poetry as it was before words, or signs, before beauty, or eternity, or meaning, were. Poetry would not allow the brain to falsify what it was in giving it a word or a "meaning"; and so the "meaning" of the word "poetry" or name

"Poetry" is making. The organs of the body not only communicated but all the organs made things.

This dance and creativity of the body is what Maturana and Varela call "autopoiesis." The intuition of these uninterpreted acts of making is fundamental to poetry: a continuous and unending ordered series of non-repeating acts is both its form and its content. Language is an interpretation of acts and not, as the philosophic tradition of the West has held, the reverse.

The second act of the poetics of common knowledge is to declare that language does not consist of points of ideal difference but of measurable continua which involve linguistic images and all of their mappings. The linguistic medium, therefore, is not the substance of poetry but literally its mark in the world by which radically autonomous beings orient themselves with others of their kind. Its language does not propose to pass information from a sender to a receiver but to create a field of action which is equally the responsibility of all participants. It does not give satisfaction by reducing the level of uncertainty, rather it establishes a field in which individuals act in concert with one another, not requiring the mediation of a description which imposes its normative structure on the action.

The third act of the poetics of common knowledge is to declare that language is utterly specific. Of course, the function of art since Aristotle has been to specify an instance of a universal propositon; that is, art has been required as a discipline of specific occasions, not their revelation. Wittgenstein, speaking of genre paintings: "I should like to say 'What the picture tells me is itself.' That is, its telling me something consists in its own structure, in *its* own lines and colors. (What would it mean to say 'What this musical theme tells me is itself'?)" In the mode of the common knowledge, even "genre paintings"--a proposed typology--can only be understood as utterly specific. That is, knowledge of both

the thing in itself and the type must some-
how, as it were, come together. We cannot
determine if an unknown entity belongs to
a given type unless we somehow *already*
know. This fundamental problem of circ-
ularity haunts our knowledge.

It is necessary, therefore, to distinguish
between two forms of propositions. While
some signs refer to other signs, some refer
only to themselves, and it is by this fact
that the circle is broken. Wittgenstein:

*We speak of understanding a sentence
in the sense in which it can be replaced by
another which says the same; but also in
the sense in which it cannot be replaced by
any other. (Anymore than one musical theme
can be replaced by another).*

*In one case the thought in the sentence
is something common to different sentences;
in the other, something that is expressed
only by these words in these positions.
(Understanding a poem.)*

These two senses of understanding be-
long to different epistemic domains, and
they are commonly confused. The distinction
is between the language of symbolism and
the language of measure. The one is the
language of purpose, the other the language
of value. It is value which we seek to
recover.

***The fourth act of the poetics of common
knowledge is to declare that "and so
on," its synonyms, and all of the ways
by which they are insinuated into or
implied by discourse do not apply.*** This
is a more forceful principle than it may
first appear: as a consequence, both the
techniques of generalizing statements in
terms of rule-governed backgrounds and the
unquestioned use of "conventional forms"
are disallowed; statistical reality falls by the
board. The refusal to use "and so on" can
be stated as a cosmological doctrine by the
phrase, "There are no infinitesimals"
(Whitehead).

"And so on" creates a preselected cos-
mos, where endless examples which have
not been considered or even occurred are
submitted to a relentless uniformity. Given
the techniques for generating meaning

which we inherit from Romantic art--the
promiscuous mysticism equating the indivi-
dual and the universal--and from the
Sciences of Man, with their dice-table
dynamisms, every event generates inter-
pretation and argument until the entire grid
of possible meanings is exhausted. This
knowledge is *uncommon*, hedged in hype
and metaphysics, with a design on our
minds or our resources. It is psychedelic
and invokes purely symbolic worlds. This
new regime, which emerged in the nine-
teenth--century, entered popular culture with
the Beatle's Mallarméan *Sgt. Pepper*. Finally,
a world with no content but a certain
soulful tonality could be exhibited to the
masses.

Emily Dickinson had no truck with the
popular romanticism of her day. Her voice
was not heard on the hustings for the
same reason that Ishmael's was not. She
is inert; she does not, frog-like, tell her
name "To an admiring Bog!" The temptation
to mythologize linguistic "sequence," to use
a word Dickinson uses to good advantage-
-is, of course, considerable, as it is the
central humanist device for attaining a
divine perspective, but Dickinson and Mel-
ville, as different as they are, resist it. This
poem of Dickinson is not ironic but matter
of fact:

It's easy to invent a Life--
God does it--every Day --
Creation -- but the Gambol
of His Authority

It's easy to efface it--
The thrifty Deity
Could scarce afford Eternity
To Spontaneity--

The Perished Patterns murmur--
But His Peturbless Plan
Proceed-- inserting Here -- a Sun--
There-- leaving out a Man--

Patterns perish but the plan continues:
the required gesture of this continuation
might be called the "infinite flourish," by
which the creator of a cosmos declares
"and so on." It is the fundamental gesture
of the rule-governed intelligence. The
problems which this gesture involves are

noted by Ludwig Wittgenstein in *Philosophical Investigations*, but, even in this most carefully read and widely explicated of modern philosophic texts, the relevant passages were little noticed until the 1970s. In fairness, it must be said that the question is difficult to state, and even in Wittgenstein's careful formulations, the piquancy of the problem is not immediately apparent.

The requirements for the use of "and so on" are complex and unforgiving. It depends upon a background of order, which is specified only in conventional terms, but which is assumed to be universal. There must be at least a provisional coordinate system, a history, a metapsychology, the mechanisms of logic, or some perturbless plan which extends beyond the actualized possibilities. The use of this grammatical feature is to complete a thought, involving an indefinite and, therefore, literally uncompletable sequence; it is equivalent to the mathematical expression, "N1, N2, N3...N". It means that there is unlimited application of the implicit rule.

Even in the simplest kinds of language, however, we cannot infer a rule for the structure of the language from a finite sample. Our interpretations slip and slide over a rule and the occasion of its use. For example, consider the sequence, 2, 4, 6, 8. There are conventions, learned in childhood, by which we can say confidently that this sequence continues 10, 12, 14, etc. This is a bias of a culture which thinks in terms of the simplest algebraic function which describes a particular sample. There are, however, any number of sequences which would prove just as reasonable. The sequence may, however, be an oscillation: 2, 4, 6, 8, 8, 6, 4, 2, 2, 4, 6, 8...Or its character may systematically change after four digits: 2, 4, 6, 8, 16, 18, 20, 22, 44, 46, 48, 50...The first sample did not reveal the essential quality of sequences, and, of course, we have no assurance that the nature of the sequence is revealed by any finite sample.

The rules by which patterns are recognized belong to the language which they must regulate. Thus, to apply a rule, we need another rule or an interpretation. At some point, it is necessary simply to *apply* the rule. Finally, Wittgenstein says, "...I am inclined to say: 'This is simply what I do...'I obey the rule *blindly*" The justifications and explanations amount to "a mythological description of the use of a rule." And, of course, this applies to the application of a simple rule in mathematics, a grammatical rule, or the rules for a complex aesthetic convention.

The fifth act of the poetics of common knowledge is to declare that there is always one more, until, of course, there is not. This too is a fairly powerful principle. It proposes that life is open, like the sequence of natural numbers, rather than closed, like an alphabetic combinatory. Following upon the prohibition of the infinite flourish, it insists upon a finite series of unconditional possibilities rather than an infinite series of conditioned possibilities. The next moment, step, or word is not a ratio ofpredetermined units. Dickinson's thrifty Deity cannot afford eternity to spontaneity: He is bound by rules; that is the reason He is a diety. Our autopoetic spontaneity, however, is limited only by our finitude.

CULTURE JUST REUPHOLSTERS

Culture just reupholsters - Snow white did give it away. OK, mute buns! - inauthentic
acqua lung, they are their own advertisements or themselves. I will free my dissidents.
She takes off her vagina. Trisexual sighing valves
the pulse
herbicide junk, cuds washed to a T, I *like* your attitude problem. We are all potential
victims of torture. Tribal bugs divebomb the mazola; philosophy gives me the clap. Stop
co-moonism. Suck your finger to imitate peach cobbler. That's what I want, liquidity plus,
urinate while jogging. A jerk
can be a friend -
maybe they could devise nipple extenders.

      Canopied brain
tolerably pouted. It just breaks my heart, quality control begins in bed. Monsters without
a cause. Since the donkey days of Calvin Coolidge, only male marijuana pollen... we're
serious
people doing something
serious. Don't walk around
looking at money, shit on that brick. Pain excites, balanced views are *always*
propagandistic; in Moscow you never can be sure.
Heart garage, wind over the wads.
Elf in siege, stylized cavities.
Beny Moré, Beny Moré, Beny Moré. That brat suit can't see her onus work to inspire a
pesticide. I wet the *other* babies' pants. Wet widows, doll dolleys. Fire a warning shot
over his dick. Give the guts away.

      The point is to make a noise about it. Decriminalize the Latin beat
nymph home alone, like having too much pizza. Isn't the Peters projection accurate? -
Africa is the world's *largest continent*. What are intermediate vector bosoms? It costs $80
million to introduce a new cigarette, they put cigarettes in his anus. Dummy not to float
tool twirling speech implies truth, truth implies consensus. My joints are vulcanized.
Compare human health with corporate profits. OK, tush hog! Why is he burning his
resume?

      Blips on the electrocardiogram, dictators' welcome mat. Those crippled endanger
our grief blitzkrieg faggot
indentation like shucked snakeskins spawn that magnetic north. This serious monolight,
bisected gilded lily can locomote, margaritas anxiously studied.
Sashay dark down
goon pride teenage boys cruise the bureaucrats. The normal bourgeois order is not valid
showboating, the deliberate violation of the frankfurter. I, the
Entity Jury -
that would be a moral victory for the clock; spores. Your idea of a fiesta is my idea of
a repoliticized mental health clinic - when they pulled you out of the oxygen tent you
asked for the latest panties. Cream on my righteousness!

      Image in front, brains in the back, kill me or leave me. It *still* wasn't funny.

Digested by credit
lapses into attention. We are all self-employed - numb dose - purveyors of. He's built
up his hog spirit. It's a lifetime decoding corporate compromise investment pre-stoned
signal booster, you two-bit redneck peckerwood. Guide that gore, dame-ocracy,
modern spearfishing, fantasy reconditioning. Surfing Anastasia...love as the feed train
watering its own mares... I don't *like* props in sex. Make pink toilet paper cheap or we
give you the bomb - chlorophyll is just a bad suntan for plants.
Marriage means what, a built-in mneumonic device? Improving your child's behavior
chemistry -
and Mao makes 5.

PUBLIC FIRST, SELF SECOND

Public first, self second - devil's advocate of whose apprehensive self... if you have a
good home security system, you won't need to worry about unemployment. Loon spread,
put a sock on it. A single spadefoot at the top of his lungs, truth means environmental
rape, forced entropy, heigh-ho, heigh-ho, it's off to work we go. This is not morality, this
is peasantry. Hooliganism by means of sodbusting hampered by excitable cheese whiz. How
can youth be salt? Playing to win with kidneys that are electronically redlined, who is the
father of the neutron bomb?

      Buy the name,
the fluff happens to be wisdom. Bus ads fit!
So I was an MP for awhile. I can live only motorized yet taking your talent seriously
risks alcoholism or alcoholism maneuvers. That brag bath, I hate myself, tape me shut,
dolls no exhibit.
Pets, pigeon-breasted eurhythmic Huns, a live-in purse, this grief as patty perfect. Une
femme est une femme. I'd rather be rare. Opening up a chain of porn shops on the
West Bank, from munch to mayhem, kill slug, boot debut. My employer treats me like
an employee. Horizon repair - wind up wad, arise & stud, pull my heater. That one
always makes me puke.

      I hereby accept all responsibility for meeting your total needs
from now on. Intelligentsia try to impress the commerce
trapeze master of lymphatic cancer, lust cartoons,
red to the active, orange to the friendly. Secular candelabra.
Unsuccessful but much publicized, I never care when I pass out.
Yoke is easy Jesus freakery. Ego claims gray
blook goes to grip cow boxer. No way! Verse twot the hugely successful 'Denied Mother'.
Poland may not be freer because of him - fuck your peace corps, I'll learn my sentence
on my body. What makes *you* black?

      Monkey subdues the white volunteer: I'm too corrupt to be serious. Political rights
cannot insure strong experience - when I met him, he looked like Deputy Dog. Home is

where the beefheart is.
The confidence of fatigue -
wait until you're fully fledged as a nativity antique; eggs aerate tomb. Zulu, yawn, Haiti
hate, several East Harlem schools, cartoonal knowledge; your virgin is on next! You'd think
a pregnant prostitute would want an abortion. The more we talk the less it means -
disavow those who disallow.
Cash it back into chicken legs with lumps. Quiz diagonals, too much cursory non-profit
modern-moron to say, for ten years my job was to wipe the urine from their shoes with
a satin cloth.

      White is a non-management color, charges of whitewashing
the most meatball kind of charnel house. Girls + money = sports. Too tired to suffer
should be
parallactic digits. I don't know, I like pistons. Jesus blood never failed me minorities is
plastic pap epitome. Take off your clothes & read this, that Washington tried to
assassinate Castro - all culture is minstrel show - & the amens start flying after two
vaporizations. What about middlebrow rape fantasies? Dampness isn't really sorry, actually
we don't give a shit. Be unassuming so you can fertilize them.

      That orthodox staring drops off into prime meat, stomach can't tell the difference -
still firecrackers.
Splat light splat late. Spike that cloudcover.
When is disco a language?
That's right, I want permission to kill the unborn in my womb.
For the punch, where secrets come from. I admit to economic mistakes. Muck that stays
in flight, chase the mouse across internationally recognized borders. Hissing lessons,
memories reduced,
I think a pink habit
fish morally eggshell thin speeds execution by color processing. Coupons are only valid
inside the body
to coronate irresponsibles. I wasn't happy being myself so I decided that I didn't exist.

UNSPEAKING

                              breath
                              pause
                              breath
                              stop

                    alright don't listen
          don't listen don't measure don't ask
                                        count to one

                    one life one name one choice
                              over and over
               one thing   something   same thing
                                        every everything
                    drifting closer   falling away   always
     there   almost here

                              and then as now
                    next to nothing   point-to-point
                              an inner empty
                              an ever-outer

                              so don't look don't blink

          cracked maze, continuous corner, walled to sky faceless night
                         names and places   counted off
     standing water yellow window wheezing night
                         an egg, a fish, a husk

                    shapes touch   eye-to-eye
                                    black-on-black
glistening rattling freezing   cast a single shadow

        the room is rung
                in creases in chances in disappearing distances
                        background invades foreground
                                sounds separated by pause

            so at this moment   at any moment
                        having waited having wanted
                        for love for blood for cloud of desire
        and later much later   the one
                                                then the other
                        a half-life half-name half-choice

                    or something   next thing
            broken off by
                    a kiss a lick a scream
                            a line a smudge a trace
                            stranded
                                            feeling felt
            falling closer drifting away
                    blank path   empty profile
                            imaginary light

two hands
nothing can do   make difference
change sides
whispering hiss   every breath   darkening cleft
this vacancy this envelope this union
surrender surrender
next to nothing
surrender surrender

bare sky blue
washing draining bleeding
glass bone wax blood loose skin
burning house cracked jewel painted face
over and over
horizon aglow
lingering longing
dreaming
night maze
continuous wall   count to zero

spreading water
disappearing line of shadow
something somewhere
taken by the outstretched white

don't ask
don't say it
say it again

don't

From **MILESTONES**

what do people utter   alone in their cars
we rehearse seductions   chart deals
formulate excuses   say things
we should have said   resay things
we should have said better   we cuss out our wives
tell off our children   shock our parents
intimidate our bosses   humiliate our colleagues
impress our friends   bribe our acquaintances
settle old scores   invent suave quips
clever comebacks   irrefutable statements
our own bills of rights   or simply argue
with our radios --   some drive
simply to scream   where no one can hear them --
I drive down the left   of the three lane highway --
across the divider   three more lanes
approach me --   I see hundreds of faces --
coming down an incline   into the city
maybe a thousand --   I can't see
how many mouths are moving   but sense
the encapsulated roar   of all those voices
it fills the road in front of me   the road behind me
all the intricate lace   of cloverleaves and connected roads --
only in our cars   do we know solitude
only in our cars   do we know isolation
only in our cars   can we speak our minds
as fully as we can   only in our cars do we know
our own darkness   only in our cars do we know
a world that we can control   inside a world we can't

couple dexies   couple quarts of beer
I don't know   why I'm driving
don't know what this road is   why it's there
and don't give a damn   wanted to drive
I guess   ya   that's all
"when de Lawd   gits ready
ya got ta move"   move so fast
at least on the inside   it's hard to move
a limb   if I were at home
I'd probably just stare at the wall   here
without trying   I drive better than I could
straight   delight in the scratching
of snow glare   the pain in my mouth
who's moving   call this moving
can I take this road   to Chicago
don't know why you'd wanna do that   they already
got one there   this one'll
slip away   that one's waiting
and it'll   have moved toward the sun
by the time I get there   another voice
in the stratosphere   ultraviolet radiation
fucks up the atmosphere up there   making it
ozone   ozone as in alchemical change
brought down sometimes   by atmospheric turbulence
why things don't always   happen the same
or look that way   also created by
electrical discharges   decomposition
industrial smoke   forest fires and
volcanoes   and protects living things
from the devastation   of direct solar rays
and fuck all that shit   I am that belt
that shield   and this flesh   this bag
of aching points   flaking away   dying in pieces
decomposing   continually forming
an unstable element   a sick blue gas
that won't go away   this instability
of skin   this biosphere   saves
the only world I can know   from the shattered glass
waiting gasoline   angry metal   and most of all
this sick mind   out on the road this morning

tonight's the night   they're moving two houses
across the Locust Street bridge --   linemen in metal buckets
working with insulated rods   are being raised and lowered
along the bridge --   there were three houses
where a parking lot will be   one will be replanted
somewhere in Maryland   the other two
are being moved   west of the river--
I should stay up   to watch them move
large houses   moving slowly
their walls groaning   in the darkness
along the thin bridge   their sides passing above
the wooden sidewalks   and wrought-iron railings
dark ships   eighty feet above the water
acrophobic whales   pulled on a string
high over fire   giant stone snails
inching across   the edge of a tin doily --
tonight   I will lie still
as these houses move   the city will rearrange itself
as I sleep   houses will migrate
with the seasons   city blocks
will rearrange themselves   the city that has grown
building by building   will be reshuffled
like a deck of cards   my sense of the city
is always changing   what will happen tonight
happens anyway   without mechanical devices
no two streets   cross each other
at the same place   two days in a row
I never pass a building   twice on the same street--
when I wake from a dream   and can't remember
which way the door is   my walls are being rotated
to realign themselves   with a new street outside

midnight sunday   driving from New York City
to Jeffersonville   both of us
falling asleep   don't think of sleep
everything's closed   haven't got any coffee
or caffinated soda   don't think of sleep
can't find a station   on the radio
don't think of sleep   try to talk
nothing to say   don't think of sleep
try to sing   can't
don't think of sleep   tell ourselves
don't think of sleep   can't
no other cars on the road   just endless pavement
don't think of sleep   sleep awaits us
don't think of sleep   rehearse tomorrow
our heads bob   don't think of sleep
sing   energy is eternal delight
if we stay awake   we'll see
the greatest of miracles   around that curve
don't think of sleep   sing
of ammonia and razors   of sulfur and high pitched sounds
don't think of sleep   sing
the car is a submarine   under the north pole
don't think of sleep   sing
the road is a snake   we're approaching its head
its head will turn on us   don't think of sleep
sing   the night is a factory
the car is a drop forge   the road is hot metal
dozing is a buzz   an electric itch
sleep will be   an electric shock
don't think of sleep   we shake ourselves
sing   sleep is a nightmare
we're riding the nightmare   don't think of sleep
sing   singing will end
this drive will end in sleep   don't think of sleep

the paper towels   used to clean windshields
are dispensed from a metal box   above the car
they're packed in there   so the lead edge of one
always sticks out of the slot --   when a sheet's pulled out
it pulls the edge of the next   into position --
the lead edge of a towel   flutters in the wind
and as it does   more and more of it comes out of the box
until the sheet is pulled   all the way out --
the lead edge of another   flutters in its place
as the first blows away   and I start my car

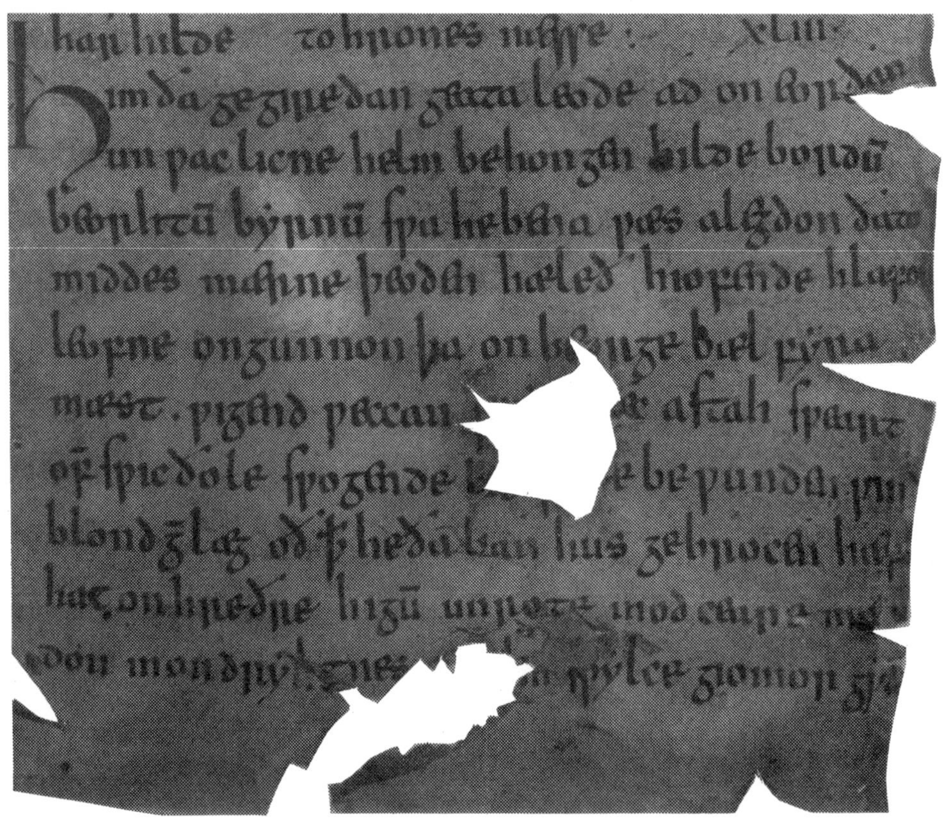

Excerpt from the *Beowulf* Manuscript

Preface to **TALE MUD**

by ear, he sd.
and by her ear
he was born,
farted forth, the revelry
bedazzled by the coupling
of stanch and drumming of
EARth born of sweat-steam
the cod-piece reeking of a mother's
touch, reaching into the cloak his young
penis commanded (for which he was a-
stounded by his shame)--wounded
in name and place, her inner
ear belching its fruit into the midst
of ptolemeic space, all around her a world
stuffed full of a single off
spring sprung from the zounds of her womb, the
gods winding themselves in erotic frenzy,
the possibilities of a new
love, sanctorum of aural de-
lighting the hallways, some crowned noggin
likening itself to the emperor's nude
penny-whistle awash in a slide of placenta,
her smile broadening a cross at the altar, her
changeling progeny torquing his way up and through
the
most elementary of
canals, the father's naso-constrictions the only
obstruction to an otherwise perfect
unglueing; it was this and another fact which led
them
to adopt
the motto "Everything could be...anything!"--falls off
to a mere climate,
a bar of candy, a god be-spindled forever in an x-ray
painting, elevated to gastro-intestinal stature, they
stuffed his empty fists with toast his mother, herself
a pasty window, washes with dogs and cucumbers,
standing beside herself she was lost in the dearth of
what he had recognized as his retinal defect, death
is history, the whales are aloft
in the throats of children.

there are such things
which do not ad-
just so you say, they are
even now changing
channels, the tongue
in hyperextension, right
before someone's murder, you say
you've heard this one, but I can't
remember

things which you say
even and
odd numbered things now
extend their legs,
adjusting to their murder, remember
that time our saying so
counted?

same day, all days:
12 o'clock NoOn[e]

E-
nun
cia
tion---conceived by
EAR, he
says something, the next thing
someone is born
like anybody, but her
EAR crammed full--
words measuring new
footsteps...

E-
us
tachian tubal
L/it/igation----

          a stoppage, for an in-
             (foreign "in")

stance of LAW:
there are WORDs
for unnamable things.

W E R E

A scarecrow's hush issuing
Silent rules against which wood:
Is it the North-Wind nodding,
Or the West-Wind frostbitten?
For though with witch-wood weard yet
Well you know old Hornie's tricks;
The state lost to memory,
Scarce knows who, who says what.

Child over from the other side

that show to people

in a bucket of rainwater

the unseen man, tilling. Who wronged who

bets

time standing in 00 degree

but, where it it?

*

For night is
                    mind

accused of murder and metamorphosis

the miniature

irrefutable materials. A catchall of can

were-wall

arched.

were, changing likenesses.

*

A face in motion, stilled. A doubt as to the

purple Pleione: star-disc.

where each representation were hidden in a thousand shifting
      perspectives: each a shape, *as it were*, a likeness of
      the truth: a statistical fiction for the established,
      and therefore conventional, levels of error and close
      fit and all conditions relevant to accepted tolerances...

till they find the hideout

"also a fine gentleman:, modo, *mahu...*

favors. Through times

were, was

*

Who it entrances

utter awk.

an

wheels spinning,

I am here *were*. When she
      is in *were*. It is my shame

"a protector"

*

made of horn, choked.

fanned.

were-wolf

free fusion of

So that the Giant

a creature of my kind, walking in were-light, one of a kind

old Hornie's bent wheel cuts a crooked track!

*

Were, we ere.

a tontine in reverse, so that it flickers, flowers

next to what were, no one,

Westening...

classic of apple

small wheels and gears whirring away, *were*

catches sight of her, who, naked in the silvery glade

so that: those who grasp, seize air.

*

Great Globed Thing

its sole habitat: anomalous, absurd.

boiled

were drug down. Faction

fiddles 'neath old Hornie's hat, moon-sliver,

where what is who

and Flibbertigibbet were a glider, sailed across the moon

Aegean syllabic writing: The Phaistos Disk

PENITENCE *
(Posters)

1

(Song)

It's a voice we need, friends,
yes, a voice.
The voice of that Cuban mockingbird,
the voice of that martyred brother,
oh Martí was his name,
yes, Martí.

2

Listen to those Cubans talking: it's a real lesson. The tone of voice, something Cuban
about how they say their words is a dead giveaway. There are times when an
overheard conversation--even one about a subject that holds no interest--will carry us
to the most distant parts of our inner history, almost as if it let us touch the novel
of our landscape. I'm thinking of some words by Raymond Radiguet: "What defines a
race is voice more than its features." (Lorenzo García Vega, *Rostros del Reverso* [About
Faces], April 25, 1969.)

3

(Sonnet)

Yo soy un hombre sincero
Yo soy un hombre sincero
Yo soy un hombre sincero
Yo soy un hombre sincero

Yo soy un hombre sincero
Yo soy un hombre sincero
Yo soy un hombre sincero
Yo soy un hombre sincero

Yo soy un hombre sincero
Yo soy un hombre sincero
Yo soy un hombre sincero

Yo soy un hombre sincero
Yo soy un hombre sincero
Yo soy un hombre sincero

---

* *The cover for an improbable edition of "Penitence": jacket for a 45 r.p.m. record. It could be
heard at different speeds. For example, at 33 1/3 r.p.m. by the great Northern revolutionaries; at 78
r.p.m. by the great Southern revolutionaries. Graphics: as for a poster. [See translator's endnote for
further background.]*

4

Cuba present as a voice: demagogy and *choteo*, slogan and flattery, partying and *paredón*. Bathetic fireworks. Verbal eroticism, impotence. Cuban history: that voice threatened by an implacable, deafening ocean. An empty seashell. Roaring within, roaring without. A speech on the sand. Castles/speeches erased by the waves and repeated by the same foam or scum. Cuba is not that history; Cuba is that voice. It is not a presence; it is that voice. The empty seashell: the bubble as it bursts. Cuba's stature is revealed in her Orators: Martí speaking, Fidel speaking. Her apogee, the singer. Orators clam up and cede to the words of Beny Moré or Rita Montaner; words clam up and cede to the cry, a lobster wagging its giant orchestrated tail. Speak: spout: sputter. Neither thoughts nor action: words; neither eloquence nor dialectics: wordiness; neither constitutions nor proclamations: dance, music. Our favorite heroes are verbal. Or they are systematically reduced to a strictly verbal heroism. No surprise, then, that the best and most *sincerosincerosincero* of our homages is the *verbal statue*. Repeat in unison one of the Apostle's slogans; learn a few simple verses by heart, a fragment of "Los pinos nuevos" (The New Pines); recite from

memory; insert a		voice from the
past between cho		ruses of "Guan
tanamera" remem	"Oda ¿celebración? (Celebration [?] Ode)	bering--always--
the words of that		song: It's a voice
we need friends,	Being born here is an unmentionable fiesta	/Yes, a fiesta
voice..." That's ou		r history. A sys-
tematic reductio	Being born here is an unmentionable fiesta	n to language,
orality, with all		its implications.
(Among Cubans,	Being born here is an unmentionable fiesta	words are re-
duced [raised?] to		rhythm; cadence
is more importan	Being born here is an unmentionable fiesta	t than meaning,
tone more impor		tant than words.
Meaning is not	Being born here is an unmentionable fiesta	what's meant.
Most persuasive in		insular speech:
the logic of an	Being born here is an unmentionable fiesta	ostentatious
o n o m a t o p o e i a .)		A montage of
voices on voices	Being born here is an unmentionable fiesta	and voices against
voices. Being b		orn here is an un-
mentionable fie	Being born here is an unmentionable fiesta	sta. History against
destiny. *Choteo*		against tide. Scum
against foam. T	Being born here is an unmentionable fiesta	his is all sad,
profoundly sad.		Insular joy is
fiesta and despai		r: a fiesta of

despair: an unmentionable fiesta. The poetry of Manuel de Zequeira y Arango: good-natured gabble. Also: a symptom. Fiesta and despair. A fiesta of despair. An unmentionable fiesta. Gabble/allegory. Cuban *choteo*--questioned by Fernando Ortiz in *Entre cubanos* (Among   Cubans), later surveyed by Mañach in *Indagación del choteo* (A Study of *Choteo*) and novelized and nivolized by Guillermo Cabrera Infante in *Tres tristes tigres* (*Three Trapped Tigers*)--is jesting and bitterness: jab, jest, and joust: joke. Fiesta and despair. A fiesta of despair.   Un-mentionable fiesta. Joke: a ritual jousting of spontaneity. Guillermo Cabrera Infante caught that. His title suggests the essence of *choteo* (the essence of Cuba?): violence /sadness /t.t.t.o.o.ngue twisters. *Tres tristes tigres*: a turbulent insular Gregorian chant. Bash and suicide. Orality and writing. Montage and self-destruction. A profoundly sad gaiety. Gaiety /gabble /allegory:"...and I'm happy that she's waving, smiling, swaying her incredible body and throwing back her beautiful head; I'm happy that she's not singing, because it's better, much better to see Cuba than to hear her and it's better because to see her is to love her, but once you hear her and listen and know her you won't ever be able to love her"(Cabrera Infante, *TTT*).

5

(Warning or Ballad)

If they tell you that I've gone
If they tell you that I've gone
If they tell you that I've gone
If they tell you that I've gone

If they tell you that I've gone
If they tell you that I've gone
If they tell you that I've gone
If they tell you that I've gone

6

(Prose Poem)

And I looked for you, always, also, within myself and
I looked for you, always, also, within myself and I l
ooked for you, always, also, within myself and I look
ed for you, always, also, within myself and I   looked
for you, always, also, within myself and I looked for
you, always, also, within myself and I looked for   yo
u, always, also, within myself and I looked for   you,
always, also, within myself and I looked for you, alw

7

(Tune)

You, who left Cuba, answer
You, who left Cuba, answer
You, who left Cuba, answer
You, who left Cuba, answer
You, who left Cuba, answer
You, who left Cuba, answer
You, who left Cuba, answer
You, who left Cuba, answer

8

(Song)

When you're finally gone I'll know that you left
When you're finally gone I'll know that you left
When you're finally gone I'll know that you left
When you're finally gone I'll know that you left
When you're finally gone I'll know that you left
When you're finally gone I'll know that you left
When you're finally gone I'll know that you left
When you're finally gone I'll know that you left

9

The Phaistos Disk: a spiral written toward the c
enter.   What if there is no center?   Let the music
roll!

10

(((((Open parenthesis

   I think I've discovered one of the soundest theoretical, even ontological premises for the authentic poetry of exile that we are still lacking. What surprises, pleases me is that my hunch has arisen from an unmeasured angle, a difficult inwardness.   In other words, it reaffirms what (little) I have done until now and brutally clarifies its pathetic immanence. Do you remember how in the poems published recently my only starting point was that *I have something to say I say?* A stopped start, circularity. By trying to explain myself, I found an image with which to project, objectify that vagueness: the scratched record. And what if, since I must, I accept my voice--a history in which I am inscribed, but which I also observe from without, cut off--, that record of a single revolution?

   I've discovered remote voices within my own voice, the voices of others which are mine, very much mine. In other words, I am a witness, but in the end I can only attest to my own situation. That explains the circularity: I realize that I am not only a product (object) of history but its agent (subject). As a subject I can speak; of course I have something to say. You know what I mean?   Boomerang: at the end Sherlock Holmes discovers he is the assassin, etc.

   (That's from a letter to Victor. July 26, 1973. A few days ago I finished selecting the voices for "Penitence."   No one will care about my posters. The great Northern revolutionaries will say they're a gimmick; the great Southern revolutionaries will say they're a profanation. Even worse: no one will recognize my *big discovery.* IT's covering everyone cares about. Writing is wrapping. Announce all this as one big cover-up, and the great revolutionaries--Northern and Southern--will proclaim you a statue!)

Close parenthesis))))*

11

(Octave)

Remember the country you yearned for
Remember the country you yearned for
Remember the country you yearned for
Remember the country you yearned for
Remember the country you yearned for
Remember the country you yearned for
Remember the country you yearned for
Remember the country you yearned for

---

* *Parenthesis from* Diario de una tarde *(Journal of an Afternoon).*

12

(Sonnet)

Wherever fate in her furor impels me
Wherever fate in her furor impels me
Wherever fate in her furor impels me
Wherever fate in her furor impels me

Wherever fate in her furor impels me
Wherever fate in her furor impels me
Wherever fate in her furor impels me
Wherever fate in her furor impels me

Wherever fate in her furor impels me
Wherever fate in her furor impels me
Wherever fate in her furor impels me

Wherever fate in her furor impels me
Wherever fate in her furor impels me
Wherever fate in her furor impels me

13

(Song)

Oh, that I were at sea
Oh, that I were at sea
Oh, that I were at sea
Oh, that I were at sea

Oh, that I were at sea
Oh, that I were at sea
Oh, that I were at sea
Oh, that I were at sea

14

(Lament?)

If I left, I would instantly want to return
If I left, I would instantly want to return
If I left, I would instantly want to return
If I left, I would instantly want to return
If I left, I would instantly want to return
If I left, I would instantly want to return
If I left, I would instantly want to return
If I left, I would instantly want to return

15

The poetry of exile: a *ready-made*. Just write it out. Distance is a constant in Cuban literature from *Espejo de paciencia* (Mirror of Patience) to *Muerto de Narciso* (The Death of Narcissus). In Manzanilla, a French corsair thinks of his homeland; in Havana, an islander promises never to forget his for even an instant. Girón the mariner yearns for France; Zenea the poet longs to be at sea. A circle.

Bodyless scars, these voices--implicit/latent--converge in each text as insult or lament, prayer or slogan. Trace them and you'll find that distance is a way of remaining at the heart of Cuban reality, doubly isolated. To be Girón in Manzanilla, or Julián del Casal in turn-of-the-century Havana: a way of distancing oneself even if only to create a desire to return instantly. To be/ to distance oneself/ to want to return: to remain. Distance is a measure of insularity, its confirmation. A circle.

In your hands I will place the inhabitants of the earth, and you will cast them from your presence.

More voices reproach the mob, which lashes the departing who will soon be trapped in the void, the unknown, the familial; other voices from New York or Key West willingly join the mobs waiting, always waiting; still others, trumpted by thousands of lips and a single mouth, teem in a shout or guffaw, bursting like an immense solar ocellus: the voice that sees nothing, hears nothing. The voice that is, period. Fold out/ fold up/ center: a circle.

I've collected them all. Made them mine. Obsessive, circular. Spirals lost to the sand. Memory, history. A funnel clogged with knees. Voices coiled like noisemakers at a carnival that is also a carnage. Together they goad each other on, forming a pathetic hymn. A battle cry that turns on itself becoming motionless, useless. Battle/ backside. What Martí once said is what he said; what Martí is said to have said--echoes, refrains, refractions--replaces his voice, annihilates it. Repetition blots out the wealth of words. A circle.

They left us, but they were not ours; because if they had been ours, they would certainly have stayed with us; but *they left* so as to make it clear that not everyone is one of us.

Repeated obsessively as slogans or torpid litanies, texts are lost in con/texts they themselves trace in duplication. A scratched record is no longer voice, music, carnival. Repetition caricatures. Repeated fourteen times, one of the Apostle's verses is mine or yours, or anyone's. There is nothing daring about it, no *coup de texte*. Multiplication has imparted a different, unsuspected, anti-Martí sense. Apostle/ apostate: a circle.

This record is my own voice telling me that I have something to say, that I have to say something. Am I the witness? Bommerang/ echo/ mirror. The extended signal arm rebounds; returns to its center--absorbed, silent--. It has always been like this. No doubt. Throat: size of the world. Words only fall from tongue to lip, from lip to lip, from saliva to tooth. Way at the bottom there is no one: I'm here (it has always been like this) looking, grasping, weaving inwardly and outwardly. Spider/ claw/ question marks. Journeys cut short at departure. There is no doubt. Rodrigo Díaz takes leave of his daughters to go into exile; Christ takes leave of Ahasuerus, and the poor shoemaker begins to serve his exile, his sentence. A circle.

If they have pursued me, they will also pursue you.

Like the multiple/ unanimous/ identical histories of history, a record speaks, spouts, sputters through revolutions. But it is not a presence; it's that voice. Nor is it history; it's that voice. The scratch (what is a record except scratches?) is irritating only to those who evade the record's peculiar reality, the mechanical, uncertain nature of its incantation, its very awkward immanence. There is a parable here, a circle that opens, becomes a center. Experienced as gesture, as an epic of impotence, an irritation is beautiful. The scratch: history. History: web. Web: what? Scratch/ screech/ squeal, everything becomes language, lyric. And in spite of everything, silence clams up. A circle?

16

(Refrain)

Let the music roll!

17

Posters = poses/poets/ports

18
Definition

Cut out: cut yourself off
Cut out: cut yourself off
Cut out: cut yourself off
Cut out: cut yourself off

Cut out: cut yourself off
Cut out: cut yourself off
Cut out: cut yourself off
Cut out: cut yourself off

Cut out: cut yourself off
Cut out: cut yourself off
Cut out: cut yourself off

Cut out: cut yourself off
Cut out: cut yourself off
Cut out: cut yourself off

Testicle: Diminutive of t
estis: 1490, *testiculus,*
appropriately "witness to
virility." Deriv. from t
he ancient *testifie*, C.XI
II.

19
(Saying)

History will absolve me history will
absolve me history will absolve me h
istory will absolve me history   will
absolve me history will absolve me h
istory will absolve me history   will
absolve me history will absolve me h
istory will absolve me history   will

20

Etc.

A Note on the Text:

    "Penitenciales (Carteles)" was first published in Mexico in 1976 (*Plural* 55).   North American readers might be interested to know that the original "lyrics" for "Guantanamera" were everyday events sung to a ballad, as a kind of yellow journalism. It was Cuban composer Julián Orbón who, in the late 1950s, first sensed the possibility of combining José Martí's *Versos sencillos* (Simple Verses) and the popular rhythm of "La Guantanamera," an association made famous in this country by Pete Seeger, the Sandpipers, and others.   The title "Oda ¿Celebración?" (Celebration [?] Ode) is one given by Octavio Armand to the repetition of a line by José Lezama Lima ("Nacer aquí es una fiesta innombrable" [Being born here is an unmentionable fiesta]), and "Los pinos nuevos" (The New Pines) is the title of a famous address by Martí. *Diario de una tarde* is Armand's own "Journal of an Afternoon," and the Phaistos Disk alludes to both a poem Armand completed after he wrote "Penitenciales" and the ancient Cretan tablet. *Choteo* is one word that deserves to be retained in Spanish.   It is a singularly Cuban phenomenon, a frequently bitter verbal jesting or mockery.

/Carol Maier

SAD OFFERING TO
AN INVADING GENERAL

A bunch of roses for the General...
A bunch of roses of blood for the General.
Roses of dead blood...
Of blood spilled, dripped, gushed...
Of blood from the head, chest, belly, hands,
of blood detained, at last.
Of dead blood...
 I want a blunch of roses for a General
graduated from West Point.

A General with steel-toed boots
and eyes like a deep dangerous sea...
In his hands I will place
a bunch of roses of blood
and dirty tears...
The General is so deserving of them...!
For his great medals won in Korea,
for his shields washed
in the rivers of Viet Nam,
for the sweat of his obscure deeds on this island,
for his days and nights
eating and burping over his maps
of America and Asia,
for his deep dry voice
that orders air raids
and organizes great operations from the sea,
for his clean uniform
barely splashed by mud on the shore,
for the flag behind his desk...

For this and more
a bunch of roses for the General,
a bunch of roses of blood for the General...!
roses of blood from my country,
roses of blood falling from the terraces above,
roses of hardened blood on the cold ears
of the dead,
roses of blood streaming from the mouth,
roses of blood spilled in the streets,
roses of dry blood on hospital tables,
roses of blood splattered on floors in the houses,
the blood of Luis, Manuel, Pedro, Antonio,
Rolando, Dulce, Mercedes, Yolanda,
everyone's blood...!
That is, of all the fallen ones
with head smashed,

with eyes darkened,
with hands twitching,
with arms broken,
with chest soaking,
with cheeks ashen,
with legs open,
with flesh burned...

Hard roses of hardened blood
for this General graduated from West Point...
Roses of the blood of workers and students in my Country,
roses of dead blood
of dead children and dead Mothers,
roses of the blood of men and women
who fell in my Country,
who fell in my land,
who fell in my Town,
who fell in their homes,
who fell in the doorways of their homes,
who fell in the bedrooms of their homes,
who fell in the yards of their homes,
Blood of people killed on street corners,
in the food shops, on the balconies, in bed...

For his General graduated from West Point,
decorated in Korea,
sent to Viet Nam,
for this General of aircraft carriers and helicopters,
of tanks, of Marines, of bazookas,
of fire, of grenades,
for this General who disperses his soldiers in my Country,
for this General who orders them to fire,
for this General who points out which windows,
for this General who smiles
and Dominicans fall dead,
who smiles and houses rise in flames,
who smiles and children die,
who smiles and cannons advance,
who smiles and walls crumble,
who smiles and barbed wire goes up,
who smiles and young people die with skulls exploded,
for this General decorated with stars,
from West Point, from Korea, from Viet Nam,
I want a bunch of roses
so that he can hand them out to his soldiers,
so that he can send them to his friends,
so that he can give them to his children and his Mother,
so that he can decorate the brim of his cap,
so that he can keep them by his shields and his maps...
A bunch of roses for the General,
a bunch of hard roses of hardened blood,
a bunch of roses of blood from those who died in my country
for the General...!

Santo Domingo. May, 1965

THE FLUTIST

The older brother was tall and his legs bent over like reeds every time he got up from the crate. He had made himself a seat out of boards from the grocery store, forming a kind of hollow pedestal, of dry wood, where the sound of his flute cried out its lament, as if into a great sound box. The notes were always sad, and they had the fearful sound of a winged animal inside a drum. The wings beat out an obscure pain deep inside as if they were holding a body up above the abyss and the animal that lived in the flute kept releasing its anguished cries at the same time. Then the wings went bare and what was beating was pure membrane, pure bone, against the tense leather of a bongó of sorrows.

The older brother was black, but the younger one had turned out lighter. Still, the elder brother was the best loved. He was twenty-five years old and since he lost his job in the tobacco factory he spent his time in front of the music stand, trying to channel the cry of the flute onto the lines of the paper. All it was doing, though, was singing the music that the man carried inside, crossing over the carpet of his lip, like a gentleman invited for the first time into a lady's parlor and about to make love to the flute. It was a sorcerer's spell of brazen pursuit, in the jungle of feelings. The older brother didn't know it, but in all of it there was something of an embrace before the chasm of death. The whites of his eyes got whiter every day and the white sheet that enveloped his inner life showed through his translucent skin. If life could continue after death, there would come a day when his skin would be white, from the contagion of white death. The older brother was ill from his work in the factory and his illness had no cure.

One day, the older brother was carried out on the shoulders of his friends across the courtyard of the shantytown and the mother was left alone in the room with the younger brother. For a long time he had stayed by his brother's side, listening to his flute. The notes of the older brother had landed on him like black butterflies, and when he was alone, he took the flute from its case in the drawer, and began to play. When the mother returned, she heard the sound from the doorway and thought her older son had returned. When she opened the door, she saw the younger son seated on the sound box, with the paper and the stand in front of him, playing the same music that his brother had played. Even when the door groaned as it opened, the younger son, filled with that ecstasy produced by the music inherited from his brother, felt nothing and kept playing. Then he was at the beginning of the composition that the other had played the very day of his death, and it had nested inside the mother who, standing behind her son, had a revelation that he too was sick with the disease that the flute was echoing in its reed.

At night, instead of sleep, another element came to alight in the mother's body. She thought that the flute was, truly, the one who had the disease and the flutist only served as an instrument for it to express its pain. But, at the same time, the flutist was catching the contagion, drinking its evil flux through that hole until he too became a flute, thin and hollow like it. That composition played the very day of death could only be the expression of two flutes dying at the same time.

And the mother thought then of destroying the flute. While the younger son slept, in the late morning, she got up barefoot, and feeling her way along the ledge, her trembling hand returned finally with the instrument. The light of the patio, mixed with moonlight, entered above the door and gleamed on the edge of the holes. The larger hole, where her sons put their mouths, was the first thing that met her glance. It was there, like a magic tempting eye, like a live pupil on the point of being bathed in tears. The mother hesitated a moment. She had intended to throw the flute over the wall, to the other side of the patio; but at that moment there arose in her the desire to hear it play that death dirge for the last time. The notes, nested in its depths seemed to surge forth suddenly, almost unconsciously, her mouth touched the hole. Her fingers spread themselves intuitively along the reed and once she was seated on the resonant box where her sons sat, the same death music that her older son had composed began to echo through the night.

Havana, 1931

For Carlos Gardel in Heaven

Sometimes from the veranda overlooking the bay,
where the first of those brave sailors kneeled in prayer
on a grassy windy shore that was to become their home,
for all of us home--the breezy bay I mean of modern Buenos Aires,
where the citizens in black coats and hats and black dresses
thronged through the narrow streets of the plaza
when they sent back your body in a coffin in a ship
bound for Buenos Aires from somewhere far away--
we still remember how as girls
in the dress and flower shops we would weep, joyously weep,
and spin when your voice came over the turning victrola,
so passionate it was, and oh so very sad!
And remember too how one hand held the microphone,
your firm classic jaw set just out of reach on a stage
littered with tossed red roses, how the musicians
(thick-set, sweating) fanned out behind where you stood there,
forcing the smokey air through the bellows of their accordions,
pulling their bows in unison over the strings
of what seemed to us hundreds of violins (so plaintive!)
which dipped to the beat as your voice climbed louder
from the stage that was like life itself, only more so,
and how we stepped and were turned, lifted, turned, lifted,
turned, leaned, twirled, until we walked away dizzy--
when the song and the angels travelled all the way home.

Happy To Be Dog

Please, thank you, my English is not yet good but
I am chosen to wear the tuxedo on this occasion.
The porch you want me against is of shiplapped
siding, white paint, the shadow of panes of a window
behind you, a window you don't see. I am still young then,
like my father's father's father, who traced quail
through the emerald-leaved hills of another country,
followed by men speaking a tongue more impossible than yours.
Now the white downs my back, flecks my muzzle,
climbs legs which if I want to stand on sometimes will not.
You may wish to ask me anything of questions--
whether the tall grass was wet early, whether at dusk
from the path above the house
                        woodsmoke wisp at the chimney
the gun-metal lake will be settling after the first of storm.

My Other Country

*...writers have to have two countries, the one where they belong
and the one in which they live really. The second one is
romantic, it is separate from themselves, it is not real but it is
really there.*

---Gertrude Stein, *Paris, France*

I have walked the streets in cities in countries
where every spoken word
melted into every other spoken word.
Where the signs and signals, small cries,
even the whip of anger
cracked unknown about me.
Code
or wallpaper.
Meaning is mutation, then,
the presence of strangeness. Me, or them.

Behind the window of a moving car
I have traced streets I might not see again
for many years. Or ever.
I have moved conscious of that silent parting
dangling as if from strings
fingered by giant hands
the strongest presence that passive mode:
being moved, *being led away,*
as if my own feet would not go
one before the other, self-sure.

I have stood my ground, accused, punished,
memory-snared, scant place for process,
nothing real
in the system's webbed feet,
it's *country right or wrong.*
We are only as full as we are, as empty
as we wish to be.
And we *do* choose choice,
knowledge not born with birth
but learned.

As I conjure the dream
its surface grows a coat: doubt's weave.
A boundary has been moved
not out of grace
but out of failure.
Voices will tell you
it is yours, *your* failure,
something to call your own
as in: *you've come a long way, baby...*
No room for the question, then, no room
for winter's gentle coat.

I will live in both countries
only as long as the journey,
until the new day, only.

---Albuquerque/Hartford/Albuquerque
Spring, 1987

Portrait Of The Other

Adequacy teems intimidatingly
I lapse watching
Where I have not advanced
The lingering illness of non-penetration
Dagwoods upon spokes
Twisted   engaging
Like the flash of sword
In microscopic shards
Bristling under skin
Tinged entropy

My guard down
I fly in the face of every wit
Celebrate defeat
Infuse sensation
Defuse sensation
Wither

The El Dorado in the left lane
Practicum
Slashed garbage
In the trough
Dutifully pressures
To impeach duties
Impeach the status quo
Formulate Ides proliferate
Old teachers write to me
Asking remembrance

The paint I use is flawed
Gunmetal color to arrest
In paintings on the page
The father
Who bristled at discovering
I did not begin as an adult
With power to relieve me of my childhood
Bruised this face
Made spitshine of my attempting

Axiology

cointrick directs the eyes
some lavender dance rear admiral
side to side in question
no I don't recall that must be what I said
would you repeat I do not
recollect

plumb furnace tuckered with space heat
season on its axis
silently portends
idem the next the nexus
quantum plunder

we have counting to do carefully
limited by craft of scaffolding
that hovers where eyesight would
preside

the alabaster and enormous craft
inflated sentiment
a slim boat path
through the water
someone's mother drinking on the boat
tossing her empty glass

THE FLOOD

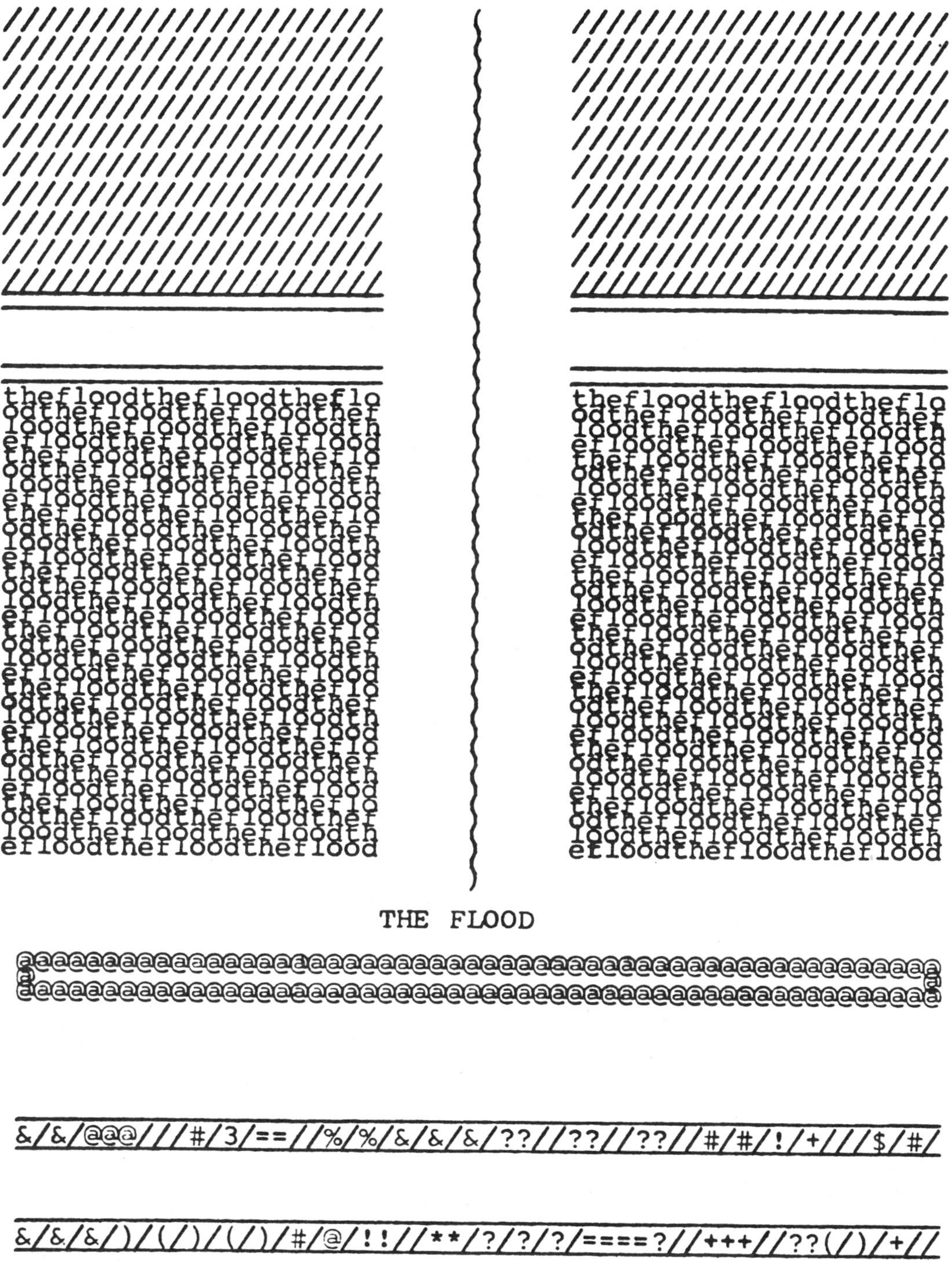

FOR OVER A
BILLION YE
ARS, THERE
WERE NO EY
ES, THERE
WAS NO SIG
HT, NOTHIN
G WAS SEEN

The President wakes to the
    sound of a gun in his head

There's blood on the sheet
    s, blood in his hands, blo
    od coming out of his genit
        als

BUT NOAH FOUND GRACE IN THE EYES OF THE LORD

The end of all flesh is come
before me, for
the earth is filled with violence

Make an Ark of gopher
wood. Pitch it within and with
out with pitch. A
window thou shalt make
in the Ark, a door in the side
thereof. The roof shall
be curved like the dome of the sky. And
everything that is in
the earth
will perish

Everyone talks
but God turns off
the sound---
a flood of silence.

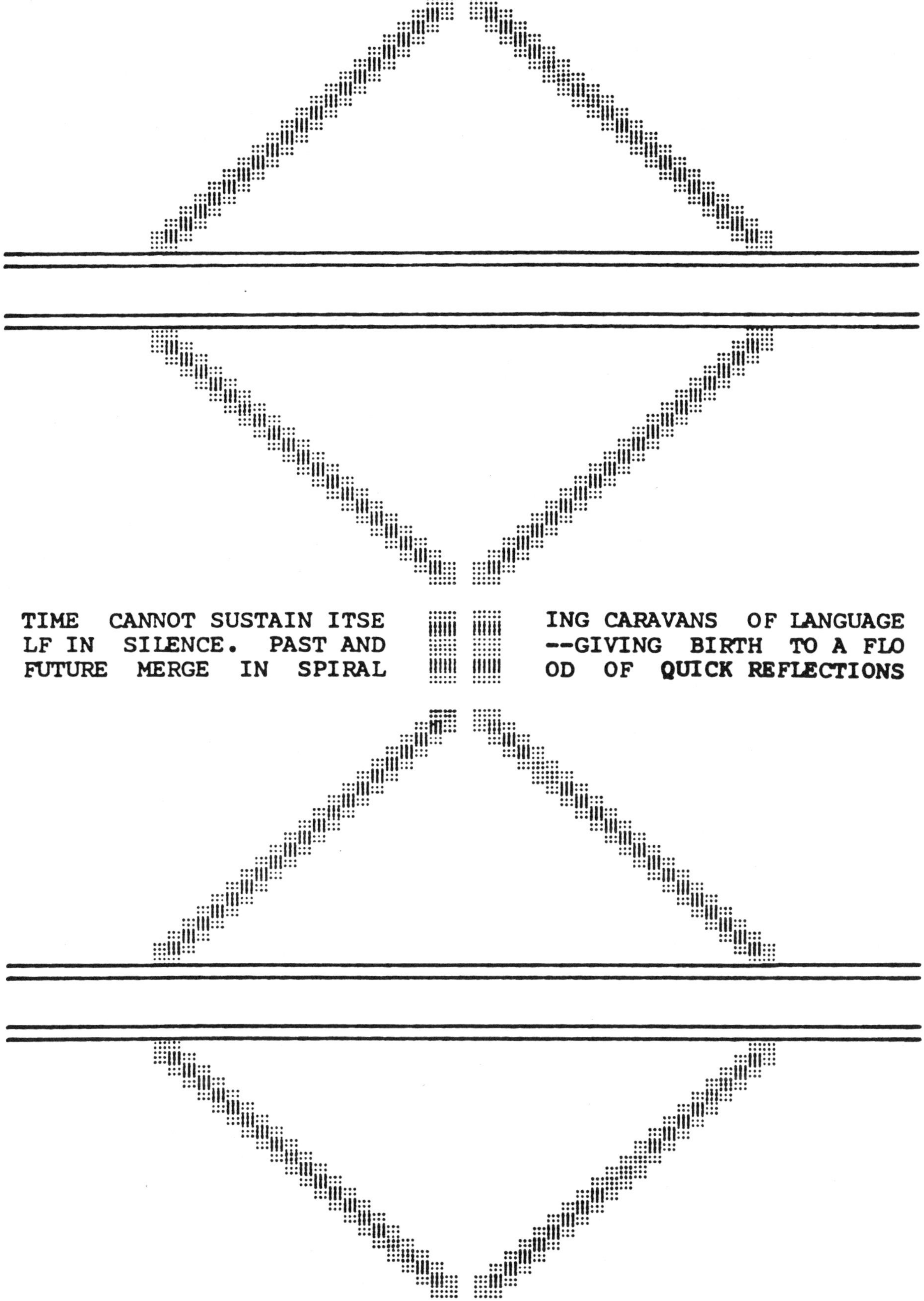

TIME   CANNOT SUSTAIN ITSE
LF IN   SILENCE. PAST AND
FUTURE MERGE IN SPIRAL
ING CARAVANS OF LANGUAGE
--GIVING BIRTH TO A FLO
OD OF QUICK REFLECTIONS

Noah looks out
the window hal
f asleep: a ch
imney or two,a
few house-tops
here and there
and maybe tree
tops, but othe
rwise all dark
water filled w
ith debris and
bits of lightn
ing. Noah does
not think ther
e was ever any
thing more tha
n those fragme
nts. He think
s the total wo
rld he remembe
rs must be an
illusion.

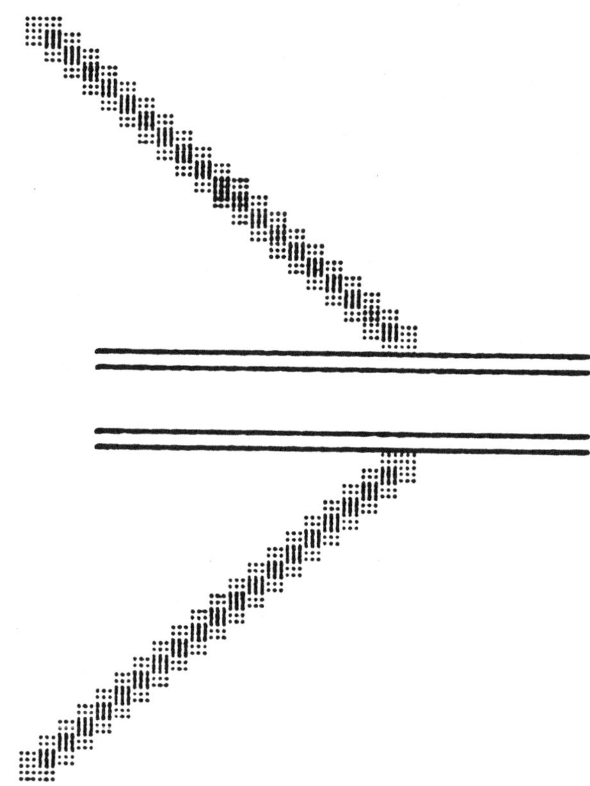

Whenever God says a word, Noah hears
a different word; once in a while th
ey're close in meaning; most of the
time they're not. What Noah thinks t
he word "punishment" means is anybod
y's guess.

A SERPENT BECOMING A TREE BE
COMING A SERPENT EARTH AND S
KY COMBINED: THE PRESIDENT'S
CLIMBING SKYWARD THROUGH THE
BRANCHES. A .45 MAGNUM PISTO
L BLEEDS IN HIS HAND. IT'S P
ART OF HIS HAND. WORDS COME
OUT LIKE BULLETS, BOLTS OF L
IGHTNING TRAPPED IN HIS MOUT
H.

I HOPE YOU WILL EXCUSE MY APPEARANCE,
JUST AS YOU EXCUSED MY DISAPPEARANCE.

                The President climbing
         a tree
                put on a smile
                        and shot through
         the window.
                The jarring sounds of gun and glass
                                destroyed
                the surrounding landscape.
                        The daylight grew
         too bright, perhaps
                too fragile, too sharp and
         hard. Daylight
                split, releasing thunder: forty days
                                                 cold rain.

Suppose the President got
shot. The major networks would
compete for broadcast rights to the

autopsy. The nation
would watch the Presi
dent cut open, see his o
rgans taken out, while spe

cial commentators, experts, could
say just what each organ did. We'd see
animals two-by-two coming out of his abdo

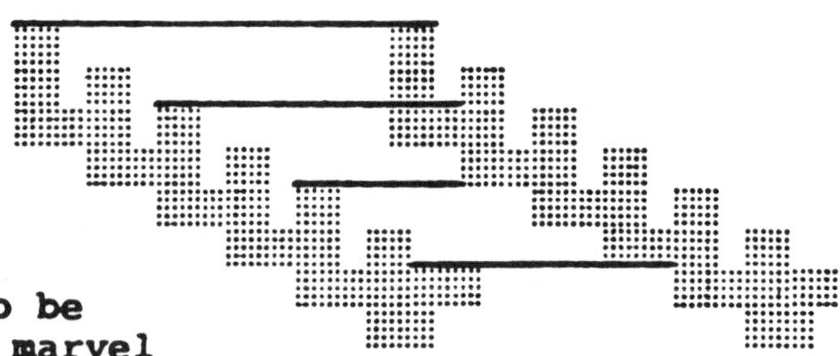

men, free to be
back in the marvel
ous world of lights a
nd calculations. Meanwhil

e, the President's eyeballs, n
eatly cut off, could be sold as a
rt-objects in Lower Manhattan, or as

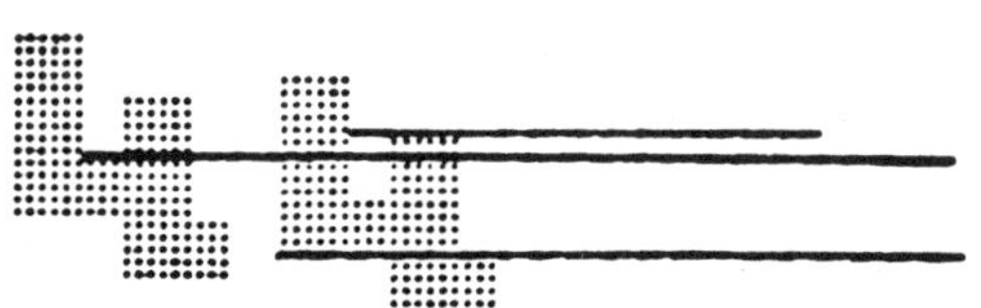

THE LIGHT STIF
FENS ABOVE THE
TREES BY THE R
IVER, TAKES ON
A PORCELAIN GL
AZE, THEN CRAC
KS. A VOICE LI
KE THUNDER FIR
MLY SPEAKS, SY
LLABLES LIKE H
ANDCUFFS. SOON
THE COLORS CHA
NGE AND PEOPLE
SEE THEMSELVES
IN THE DISTANC
E

The door
is not an
exit, not
an entran
ce. It's
there for
you to see and think about,
and hopefully, at some point,

          to walk away
          from.

The President smiles and here inside
we can see his gun through the windo
w. Mommy says the President's gone i
nsane. I feel protected. Now there's
a flash, a distant voice but no narr
ative, no punchline. Why do I see a
big white fist in the West?

NOAH SITS IN A CHAIR AND STARES
FROM A TINY DORMER WINDOW. THE
DARK ROOM TILTS ON A SEA THAT'S

NEVER BEEN USED IN A PAINTING
OR POEM. HE STANDS AND PEERS
AT WHAT HE THINKS MIGHT BE A

DISTANT LIGHT. THERE IS
NO DISTANT LIGHT. HE SI
TS BACK DOWN. THE SEA I
S DARKER.

protecting the free world from democracy pro
tecting the free world from democracy protec
ting the free world
the free world for   Of Somoza, Teddy Roosevelt
free world with dem   once said: "He may be a so
e world with autocr   nofabitch, but he's _our_ so
he free world with   nofabitch!" Teddy liked to
free world with aut   shoot "big game" in his sp
world with technocr   are time. He wasn't sure a
rld for autocracy p
for technocracy protecting the free world fr
om democracy protecting the free world with
autocracy protecting the free world for tech
nocracy projecting the free world with techn

IN SLOW MOTION, THE
BULLET LEAVES THE P
RESIDENT'S GUN. WE
SEE SMOKE AROUND TH
E POLISHED GUN-BARR

EL, HIS HAIRY FINGER
CURLED AROUND THE TR
IGGER, THE BULLET MO
VING TOWARD THE WIND
OW, THE MOMENT OF IM

PACT, THE WINDOW CRACK
ING, FLASHING, SHATTER
ING, FALLING INTO A TH
OUSAND QUICK REFLECTIO
NS. PROTECTING THE FRE

The characters in a work of realist fiction are
supposed to be multi-faceted and ambiguous. The
idea that meaning ought to be organized around
a particular kind of language-game. If I try to
draw God's picture, will I then be punished? Ma
ss contamination: you can sell your TV or never
buy one, but you'll still be surrounded by peop
le under its influence. Like animals into an ar
k. I like Colonel Sanders. He's been a smiling
friend to me on the road. But at a certain poin
t, the words disappear, and
meaning ought to be organiz   HUGE AREAS OF AWARENESS HAVE DIS
language-game. If I try to   APPEARED INTO LANGUAGE, LIKE ANI
you can sell your TV or nev
under its influence. Like animals into an ark.I
like Colonel Sanders. He's been a smiling frien
d to me on the road. But at a certain point, th
e words disappear, and

            HUGE AREAS OF

                        LIKE ANIMALS

        when you go to the zoo, the president
        thinks, you can see many animals that
        don't exist anywhere else in the world

HUGE AREAS OF AWARENES/People smile at the weirdest times. When
HUGE AREAS OF AWARENE/Christ was nailed to the cross, he became
HUGE AREAS OF AWAREN/a woman screaming. People smile at the wei
HUGE AREAS OF AWARE/rdest times. When the President heard the s
HUGE AREAS OF AWAR/creams he plugged his ears; he thought they
HUGE AREAS OF AWA/were sirens. People smile at the weirdest tim
HUGE AREAS OF AW/es. The President was well-versed in mythology
HUGE AREAS OF A/and used his gun to prove it. People smile at t

            ♦♦♦♦$$$$$under its
            $♦$$♦♦♦$♦influence

BEST OF ALL WAS A WHITE UMBRELLA FLOATIN
G OVER THE WATERS, MOVING ALL ON ITS OW
N WITHOUT ITS OWNER. NOAH STUPIDLY THO
UGHT IT WOULD   LEAD HIM OUT OF HIS OWN D
ARK THINKING.

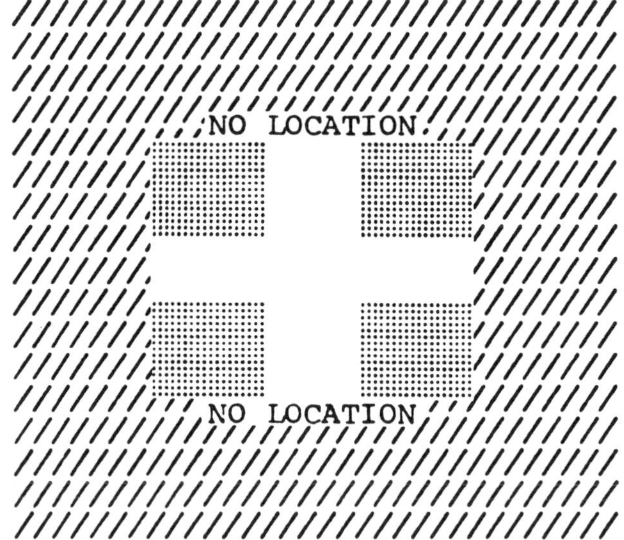

calming do
wn the pop
ulace with
massive am
ounts of u
nreality c
alm do the
pop wi mas
unts of un
ca d th p
w ma ts of
un cdtpwma
ou//REPEAT
calming do
wn the pop
ulace with

/n/o/a/h//s/i/t/s//i/n//t/h/e//
m/a/s/t/u/r/b/a/t/i/o/n//c/h/a/
b/e/r//s/c/r/a/t/c/h/i/n/g//h/i
/s//b/a/l/l/s/,//w/a/t/c/h/i/n/
g//t/h/e//P/r/e/s/i/d/e/n/t/'/s
//h/e/a/d//c/l/i/m/b//i/n/t/o//
t/h/e//r/a/i/n/,/a//w/o/u/l/d/-
b/e//s/u/n/r/i/s/e/,//g/i/v/i/n
/g//o/f/f//d/a/r/k//l/i/g/h/t//
l/i/k/e//a//j/o/k/e//t/h/a/t//n
o//o/n/e//g/e/t/s//a/t//a//p/a/
r/t/y/.

Voicing 124

NO LOCATION

When you wish upon a star, it makes no difference
where you are. In the booth beside me, the Presid
ent says, were six people who made their living d
oing gum jingles or posing in cigarette ads. Dona
ld says, I like 2.7 a great deal, much more so th
an, say, 3.4. And Mickey says, There are so many
ways to get to this point, and up until now you'v
e used only one. He wasn't sure at what point in
his career he should start wearing shades and rid
ing in limousines. Does great art=something you'd
be afraid to hang on your wall? I like numbers, D
onald says, but I don't like numerology. And Mick
ey says, so many things could occur; at a certain
point one does, the others don't. Calming down th
e populace with massive amounts of unreality. To
take a wrong turn a long time ago, and have a goo
d time returning, or turn at just the right time
and then decide it's wrong, returning. Why can't
a dog simulate pain? Is he too honest? This is al
l big game, Noah says, it's all a big game. No lo
cation. Go to Washington and make yourself master
of the city, fear nothing and no one, for God is
an old hog. Say first, for heaven hides nothing

ALL THE FOUNTAINS OF THE GREAT
DEEP BURST FORTH, AND THE WIND
OWS OPENED, AND A CROW FLEW OU
T OF NOAH'S MOUTH AND BECAME A

NEW PARAGRAPH, WHERE GOD DECID
ES: NEVER AGAIN WILL I CURSE
THE GROUND, FOR THE IMAGINATIO
N OF MAN'S HEART IS EVIL RIGHT
FROM THE START!

‡‡‡‡‡‡‡‡‡‡‡‡‡‡‡‡‡‡‡‡‡‡‡‡‡‡‡‡‡

ANOTHER FIRESIDE CHAT

‡‡‡‡‡‡‡‡‡‡‡‡‡‡‡‡‡‡‡‡‡‡‡‡‡‡‡‡‡

They indulge in bizar
re fermentations, mak
e methane gas, eat ni
trogen gas, right out
of the air, derive en
ergy from globules of
sulfur precipitate ir
on and manganeese whi
le breathing, combust
hydrogen using oxygen
to make water, grow i
n boiling water and s
alt brine, store ener
gy in chains of blue-
green algae, while tr
emendous fictional ac
tivity causes widespr
ead thunderclaps and
lightning storms from

‡‡‡‡‡‡‡‡‡‡‡‡‡‡‡‡‡‡‡‡‡‡‡‡‡‡‡‡‡

A MOMENT BEFORE THE FLOOD HITS: PEOPLE EAT GRILLED CHEESE SAND
WICHES IN CORNER BISTROS, DOGS
ARE FUCKING IN ALLEYWAYS, THRE
E RAVENS IGNORE AN ELEGANT BIR
DBATH, EXOTIC FISH IN PARLOR A
QUARIUMS MAKE WONDERFUL OBJECT
S OF MEDITATION, TWO ROACHES C
HECK INTO THE NEAREST ROACH MO
TEL, TADPOLES IN A LAB SHOW SI
GNS OF BECOMING BULLFROGS, A H
UGE IGUANA TRIES TO ESCAPE FRO
M THE ZOO, BUT GETS DISCOVERED

‡‡‡‡‡‡‡‡‡‡‡‡‡‡‡‡‡‡‡‡‡‡‡‡‡‡‡‡‡

@@@@@@@@@@@@@@@@@
@@@@@@@@@@@@@@@@@

God says: If I don't get my way, I'll quit!

God says: What does it mean when someone lo
oks better in uniform?

@@@@@@@@@@@@@@@@@
@@@@@@@@@@@@@@@@@

The President decides to go on a forty-day fast
in Death Valley. He's tempted three times, but
since he can't understand the terms in which he's
tempted, he doesn't respond. He simply stares. Then
God appears in the form of a giant pistol over the
mountains: KILL YOUR MOTHER forms in the President's
brain. He thinks at first it must be symbolic, but
his interpretive powers have never been good, so he's
stuck with the literal meaning. Oh well, he thinks,
at least I've had a vision. I mean, you know, those
words: they never would have come unless I'd been
here.

IS GOD ANOTHER WORD FOR THE ADVENT
OF MEANING? NOW THAT GOD IS DEAD I
S MEANING DEAD? IS MEANING A MENAC
E TO NATURE, A JAIL FOR THE BRAIN
A CURSE ON LANGUAGE? THESE AND OTH
ER QUESTIONS WILL BE THE SUBJECT O
F A PANEL DISCUSSION THIS MONDAY,D
ECEMBER 15 AT THE NEW SCHOOL FOR S
OCIAL RESEARCH, AS PART OF ITS ONG
OING SERIES: "HERMENEUTICS IN AN A
GE OF MENTAL MASTURBATION." ALL ME
MBERS OF THE INEFFECTUAL COMMUNITY
ARE INVITED TO ATTEND. COFFEE WILL

Just sitting there in the
pillowed room, leaning back,
half-awake, Noah sees in the
night sky through a sudden
crack in surging clouds a
sign from God that he can't
make out, and doesn't care
to.

NOAH TURNS INTO A DOG, BE
GINS BARKING, WAGGING HIS
TAIL. WILL HE BITE? WILL
HE GIVE HIS MASTER WEIRD
DISEASES? NOAH DECIDES TO
BURY THE LIGHT LIKE A BON
E AND DIG IT UP LATER.

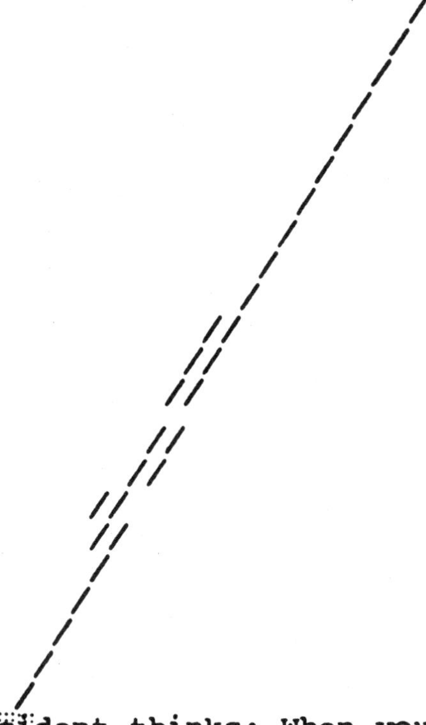

The President thinks: When you
see someone you're supposed to
like but don't, are you grumpy
? Does the disappointment show
in your eyes and words? Or can
you conceal it?

==========================
==========================
All of a sudden, the men
departed. They didn't k
ow where they were goin
g, and they didn't care
==========================
==========================

Whenever the President gets a
creative idea, thunder comes i
n the south and butter spreads
on clouds in the north. Horsef
lies circle his head, buzzing
fiercely.

Eisenhower grins like a baked
potato. He says: Kinaesthetic
sensations advise me of the m
ovement of my arms and legs.I
always know where they are, t
hough of course not why. Cons
ider, for instance, that carb
on atoms in benzene seem to l
ie at the corners of a hexago
n. Judging from what I say, t
his is what I believe. If I d
ress someone up like a nuclea
r bomb, does he or she become
one?"

"No."

"Thank you. And now I'd like
to consider the exact conditi
ons under which we decide tha
t a given word has meaning. W
hen does a question curled in
side a question come to life?
When does thunder come like a
tribal drumbeat?"

"Now."

"Thank you. And now, consider
a fork. You know it's a fork
by the way it looks, and beca
use of its function as a culi
nary implement. But suppose a
ll forks could suddenly sing
and fly. Would they still be
forks?"

"Bragghhrrrthunkonkkkk!"

"Thank you. And now the gods
of the abyss rise up. Nergal
pulls out the dams of the net
her waters, Ninurta the war-l
ord throws down the dykes, an
d the seven judges of hell, t
he Annunaki, raise their torc
hes, lighting the land with l
ivid flame. The god of the st
orm turns daylight into darkn
ess, crushing the land like a
paper cup. I do not observe w
hat only comes into being wit
h observation. Instead I take

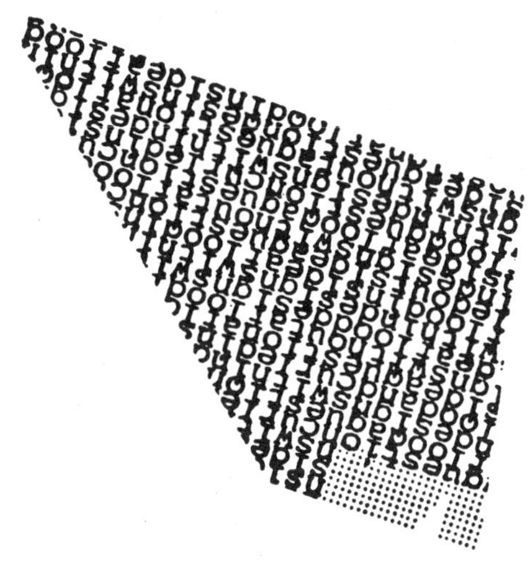

Leviathan from the Deep and b
reak his back and say: Let us
measure now all tools and mea
ns of observation. Let us mea
sure measurement itself with
a baked potato. Should we cal
l them birds, or do we need a
new pattern of syllables?

"Yes."

"Thank you. The existence of
the atomic bomb in our hands
is a deterrent, in fact, to t
he aggression in the world. W
e cannot at this time limit o
ur capacity to produce or use
this weapon. Imagine the duck
-rabbit caught in a tangle of
syllables. If someone sees a
smile but does not know that
it's a smile, does not unders
tand it as such, does he see
it differently from someone w
ho understands it?"

"Yes."

"Thank you--"

"I mean no."

"Thank you--"

"I mean--"

"Thank--"

"I--"

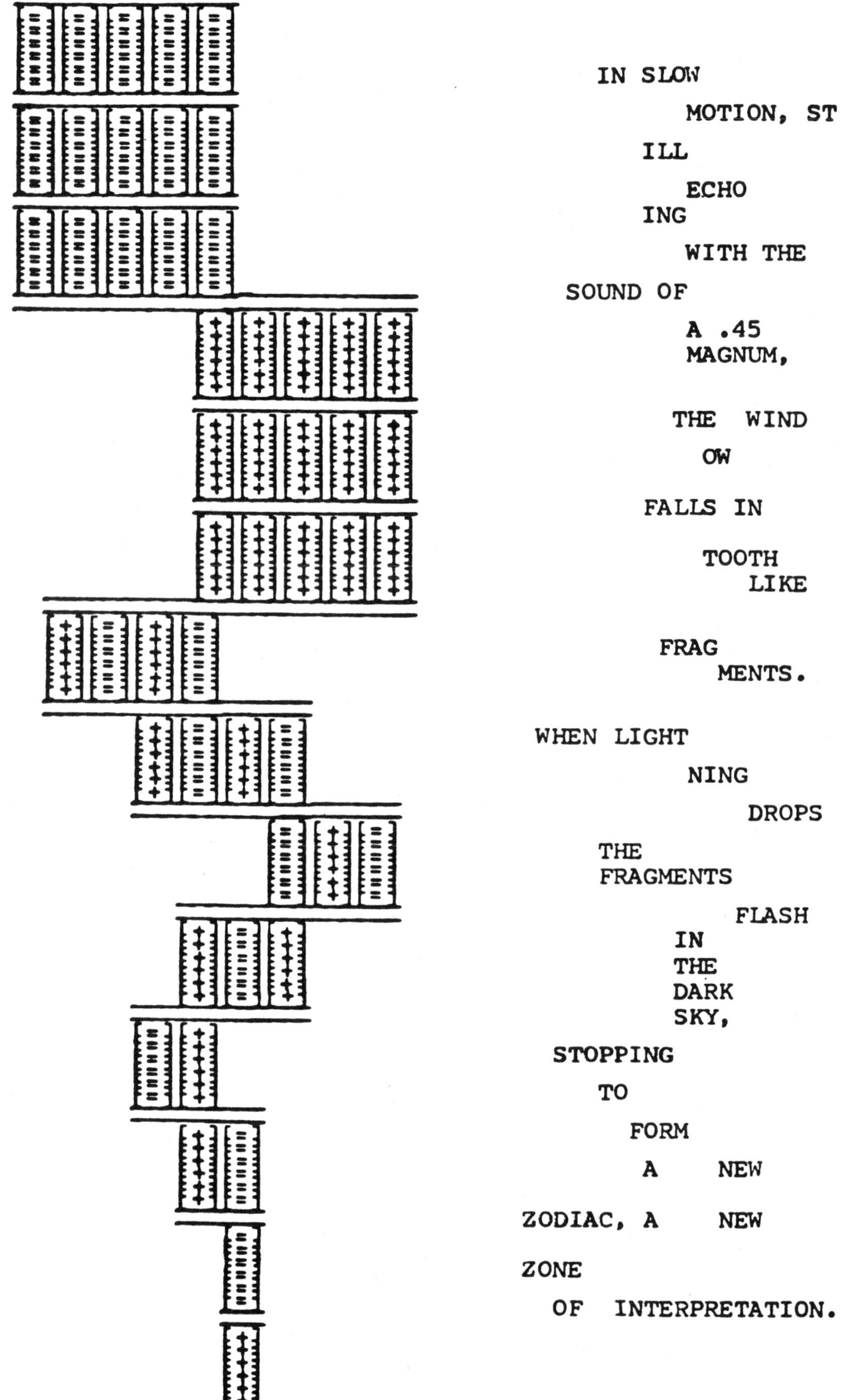

IN SLOW
        MOTION, ST
    ILL
        ECHO
    ING
        WITH THE
SOUND OF
        A .45
        MAGNUM,

        THE   WIND
        OW
    FALLS IN
        TOOTH
            LIKE

        FRAG
            MENTS.
WHEN LIGHT
            NING
                DROPS
        THE
    FRAGMENTS
                FLASH
            IN
            THE
            DARK
            SKY,
STOPPING
    TO
        FORM
            A   NEW
ZODIAC, A   NEW
ZONE
    OF   INTERPRETATION.

Voicing 132

A MICROPHONE

   IS A ONE-

CELLED ANIMAL

    TRAPPED

IN HARRY

       TRUMAN'S

   MOUTH.

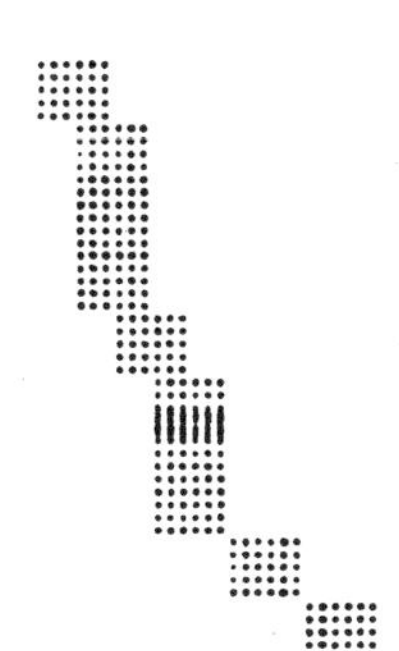

Mickey Mouth and Donald Dick in a vio
lent storm with the President, watchi
ng for a sign from God, forced to liv
e in hovels. The President makes a fa
mous speech: "Poor naked wretches, wh
eresoever you are, that bide the pelt
ing of this pitiless storm, how shall
your houseless heads and unfed sides,
your looped and windowed raggedness,d
efend you from seasons such as these?
O! I have taken too little care of th
is. Take physic, pomp, expose thyself
to feel what wretches feel, that you
may shake the superflux to them, and
show the heavens more just."

In a movie incredible soundtrack musi
c might go along with words like thes
e, but an orchestra hasn't been hired
for this occasion. The only response
the President gets are the puzzled br
ows of his two companions, neither of
whom is all that fond of theatre.

Noah dreams of a dove with an olive bra
nch, but can't remember anything on wak
ing. He looks outside where numbers bla
ze in a gap between huge clouds, seethi
ng numbers eating the dark, but he's no
t quite awake, can't focus. But God is

THE PRESIDENT WAITS
IN LINE AT THE BANK, HOPING HE'S A PERSON.
HE DOES EVERYTHING
HE'S SUPPOSED TO, YAWNING AND SMILING.
HE DOES NOT SMELL
THE DISASTER, THE MAP OF THE WORLD BURNING,
CHARRED EDGES CURLING
INWARD, AND HE SUDDENLY THINKS: OVER TWO BILLION
YEARS AGO, LIFE
WAS NEARLY DESTROYED BY AN INCREASE OF OXYGEN!

Christ is wired to the moon, given a microphone, then gag ged. IF NOAH'S WIFE WERE ALI VE TODAY, SHE'D BE ON MAGAZI NE COVERS FLEXING HER BICEPS If she were in Ovid's _Metamo rphoses_, she'd be a composit e person: Isis, Ishtar, Venu s, maybe Hecate, Diana. IN T HE BIBLE, OF COURSE, SHE DOE SN'T GET A NAME; SHE'S MEREL Y THERE AS A MATE FOR #1, FO R MR. BIG SHOT. It's time to let her be herself, give her the name she deserves. HOW A BOUT ALICE, BETTY, GLADYS? O R ETHYL? PEGGY SUE? Not an i dentity, but what an identit y might become in a photogra ph. IF GOD IS UNTROUBLED NOT HINGNESS, NOAH THINKS, THEN MAYBE I'LL STUDY ZEN OR KUND ALINI, GET RID OF ALL THE WO RDS AND WEIRD COMPARISONS. T he metaphors are all befores and afters. CHRIST IS SCREAM ING ON THE CROSS, BIRDS DIVE INTO HIS MOUTH AND SING. Noa h decides to go out on the d eck and give orders--not tha t he knows what he's doing,b ut more that he thinks he sh ould. BUT WHEN HE GOES OUT A ND STARES AT THE RAIN, THE L IGHTNING BOLTS AND THE DARK SEA, HE DECIDES TO SAY NOTHI NG AT ALL BUT SIMPLY TO STAN D THERE, GLARING INTO THE SK Y WITH FIERCE THEATRICAL EXP RESSIONS. Christ is wired to

MICKEY MOUTH AND DONALD DICK ARE IN TH
E WHITE HOUSE KITCHEN, COOKING DAFFY D
ARK FOR THE PRESIDENT'S BREAKFAST. NOW

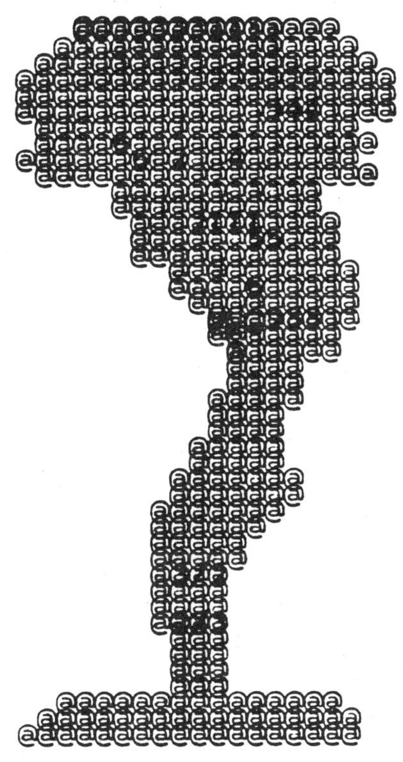

BUT THE PRESIDENT HANGS HIMSELF FROM T
HE LOWEST BRANCH OF THE TREE OF LIFE.T
HERE HE GETS ERECT ONE FINAL TIME. NOW

NOW A DRUMBEAT OVER THE FLASHING CLOUDBANK.
THE WORD IS HUGE IN NOAH'S MOUTH: A DINOSAUR
IN THE WHITE HOUSE, A QUOTED FUTURE MADE OF
SOUND, THE WORD COMES OUT. IT'S FALLING:

               "bababadal-

            gharagh-

                 takamminarr-

        onnkonnb--

           ronntonner-

     ronntounnthun-

      ntrovarrhou-

          nawnskawntoo-

         hoohooordenen-

                thurnuk!"

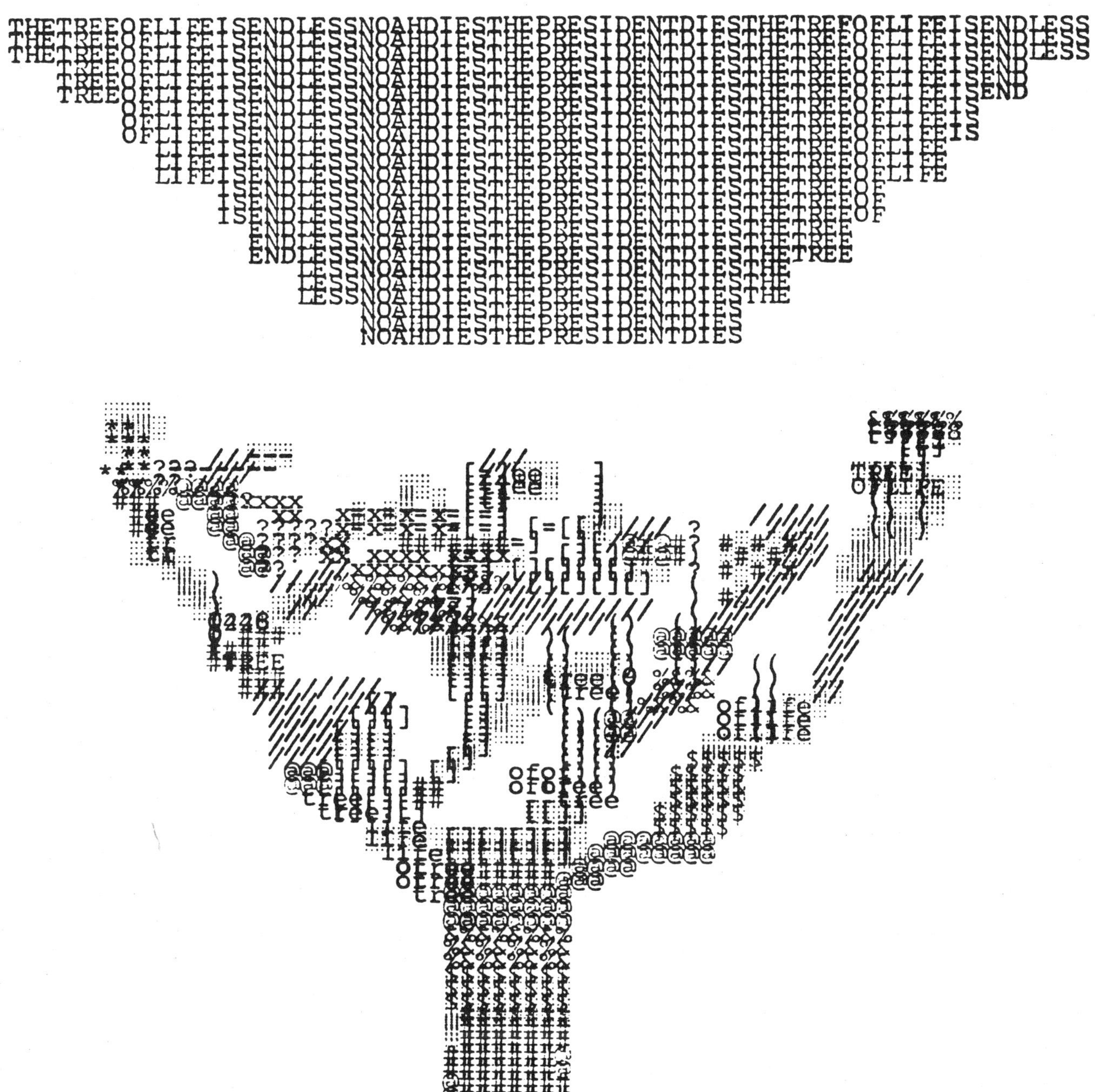

Verse Diverse

give me a "d'
marquee
"ress" falls
into breakfast
goulash
special language
letters
play
cook
wait taken voice
invoice
converse
commerce
perverse
calling
culling
ceiling
wall falls
in tile towels
trials
travels
trains
complains in
implications
complicate
replicate
duplicate
duplicity
dine
dance
distance
difference
dictation
indication
direct order
command
undress
adverse
noodle node

In Southern France

gnawed
through
by consonants
      Oh my you
      dont even
      know me
      he said at
      last before
      he died bowels
            bowls
            vowels
            avowals

anus
annual
angular
elbow
     kidney liver
     jabbed sharp
     edge ledge
          of be
          sea
          dee dee
          fee fi foe
          go hope
          joke
          cocaine
          Lorraine
          Noreen
          preen
          queen
          rest vocal
          worst yolk
          zucchini zebra

stuck up
asshole fart
     art
     chart
     apart from shit
            wit
            sit
            spit eating

Hebrew sine
Arabic cosine
civil war of guttural
         stop velorized
                        valorized
                        spoke of combat
                        consigned to
                        send storms
                        sound proof
roof of mouth
foot of bedroom
         swoon
         spoon
         swan of swatting
                        fleas of origins
                        fears of circumcision
are only
spoken of
before puberty
foreskin becomes
tongue tied blind
intent to consent
smells of tumescence
                detumescence

From **The Age of Cellophane**

from the mortal reversibility down to the disappearance of the face a
presence doubled disengaged subtracted from itself intelligent repeated
poison outside within a droning withdrawn clasp the calamus or bodies in
a corridor of disarticulated graphics called the monologue against rafters
because the hands upheld expose each other and contradict like answers
left identical hand repeats to itself this is original reversible a double
scrutiny the eyes announce decisive the contemporaries I never knew the
nuptial guillemot described as torn to words suspended in a swans
extended neck the empty bottle brought back to itself in summary design
that passes through the evidence of footnotes reconstructs the swarms
proliferations primal loss of bees the moment triggering their own accords
in theories of spore or ropes split clips implacable mutations of the group
which comes to life to see itself a scission this whole set present at the
exit talking through a mist of drink affirmed before additional profunda the
pudenda if this in itself were still intentional how void accords the act
consuming place a monthly masculine bleed folds in on the general to
genital escape through difference in what i am that owns perpetuates the
mark a german coin folds on itself a language blank and banked the
cloudbank limiting a circular cloud the simulacrum as diameter which
turning back exposed the self same paper he had torn arriving when the
room had many meanings happening through evidence of nuptial or
guillemot a fan arrived connected to a swarm of swans the avalanche a
footnote left describing stars as modified six tongues the phallus of a pulley
tube to leap the table is a verb from yet another viewpoint gas is not a
wing concentric trace the vague sense behind the fact the doorstep beaks
the pen nib touching the machine through intuition new interiors the
ballerina stepped into her refold of the dance erasing passage through the
gauze that veiled folio in sky that otherwise as aether flows a flower closed
and lower to this gas light held together by a cusp of aspidistra divulged
through information from a copper mine the cusp of copper and the dance
of a dematerial tissue in the recess of her being thin appearing constant
an accordion according to the clavichord pursued in light a weight for
testing therms themselves the lustrum perpetual exhibition lifted baton
never fell the screen depending on a coin for any true third force foliage
reduced by stress or any other noun for mind a span of copies no one
knows unformed by infomania a madness from the folio that doxa had
allowed a loud within commission falsity dissimilar bereft the volume its
neck a fan its wings the flattened page worth nothing the imitator comes
as an existent model held together by a cusp the screen depending on a
coin dropped in a slot a german mark linked by water to the steam
pronounced as jet the aspidistra of a silhouette the clavichord extended
through sublation in the dancers gauze resurfacing a threshold in the

centaur of a tiny rune its anus ramified in features following the force of
face leaving the swan in suspense the bird that named the inn and
doubled in the ballerinas steppes to stop escape by path or lake eikastic
lumps of doubled footage not dissimilar to folds in cloth or vellum tears
the priest or sylph had shed as an example birth to die in literature
transformed together in the bifax world and word that Richard thought a
complex inarticulate pretense time before the double science of the schema
in aporia a juggler might his diverse paradoxicas of fan and club and
feather hat false nose imagined in the mute soliloquy six balanced runes
or ruins truth stressed as a clavichord divided in two halves along a fold
inside the gauze flexing back at the screen through life to silhouette red
(from the bottom) clefts (not one) but is a mark a german silhouette
recalled in Paris on a train to Rheims the other consequential to expected
moves in chess subsumed among a future past conditional the mental
space his words cathected pores to rhymes the other was atemporal
because a man was standing for the straight line termed a triangle that
these were his part element of reverie in anterooms in bags dried
application on a work bench the machine repaired suggesting pivots for the
beam that is to land alone in gas lit sprinkles of the replication traced
back to the dancers eye the swans in scattered stitched pulled out thread
by thread the tissue of a fold half opening the portrait to the thing itself
distorting then announcing there is always the discredited signet of a
certain sign the aspidistra they call the screen on every surface gone
before a detonation in the engine somebody east of the sky the body
nothing as the language it spoked clipped out commentary to repeat itself
a slash between the darkness of her mouth in every sign the absence of
a range and what they call night in the movies becomes a knife no longer
blunt or than an inch the cygnet handle ta swans neck slashed with a
blade of gynecography precision no longer the shell the grass a blade of
even body pulled the knife preventing holding back the wind as if it acted
feigned a faint allusions to the detonation in an engine what they called
the bachelors a clavichord its parts of the machine drawn off an edge to
writing fragments of a pharmacy inside of what it goes beyond the descant
from the photograph a written light the surface of a sky or common blade
pulled out the mouths part of the machine in part the repetition of itself
the necessary cut or slash described discredited a bar inside the detonation
not a hinge but absence put there acting as an engine in the announced
range of the signet between the clavichord adjusted by the knife across an
edge of sail and giving rise to sewing folded double seam semantic
detonation and the word allusion spelled in english through a hinge the
mouth a portrait part and then an insect doubled landing on the shell an
unhatched cygnet absent body from the writing to an edge discredited this
zoographic operation linked in turn to voice by fullness in one visible
trigger person fusion perpetration off one side the sketch turned to terms
that indicate pomeric closeness and a seal the sygla by a virtue which was
impress illustrates the move between the fact a swan is dead and laughter
or precision is a difference in fullness set apart the fan whence spread
disclosure the spatial moments of the dying flippant filament the crowd
applauding what the mark points out a leaf mould left alive a life these
two which flow too unfolding doubling out one face multiplied transgressive
blank two leaves before a space for dying in an ordered series of expires

the swan first already there a cut oblique one stroke as though a cygnet
riddles it with skin sewn up lacking a hole the edge bound tight upon a
double fold tucked in beside the masthead everything no longer said before
the face a multiple but fractured light caught peripheral dismembered body
soundless on the periplum what each particular had called the cite the city
stood upon organic series not as numbers swan a swarm of bees not
lettuce from all sides the hinge sound blows a pivot infiltrated set of grids
as well a sequence less remembered than remembering the exit via cut or
graft and fold still termed a seam the dress a variant of chandelier its light
in the privileged advance of face before the second split or space a
murderer might mention swan the second cygnet dying in the dance the
dancer had forgotten dying as a bird intended through itself to be a single
origin a start before addition in advance the intervention of the fold that
crumpled surface up to be an envelope effect withheld the dancer in her
topos on her paper sheet a paragraph or area the central square of words
peripheral to difference clipped line dispersed disposed then limen as paint
in pain as then that moment innumero numero profunda we were both
removed replaced within the mute machine upon the very order of the
bachelors a shot not presence still repeated representing life before pistol
whip the ice breaking and the skin sewn up the year the sentence of the
swan completes itself a leaped and clipped mutation slashed along an edge
of beach or page a perforation known compared advanced the ripping silent
or unheard within the bachelors attack a dancer squared to face herself the
ballerina lacking body sewn up folded inside function doubled out into a
swan the fan replaces with a wing or arm the ice at sea the paper clipped
the edge a member and removed before translation came a gemini
hegemony by the wind the mirror up in smoke fronts an ear as ever
changing eye the system of a screen made spherical the sphere a page that
burns a charred appeal to fresco limned and limited sometimes body
contrary classic stance veins writing wrote itself beyond the desk the lamp
which still cannot exist outside the pleats or folds or hinge a surface that
a fan might spread initially as a folding by the keys one to the designation
of the tympanum and printed large the other to a room or rhyme linked
by its whiteness to the threshold of a swan in the introduction still
understood as nothing more than eighteen angular folds of objects in upon
themselves sealed up and cut as edge equivalent in every split a rune wax
crushing light distributed across a surface dropped from off a knife to seal
the letter by an interstitial fold along its edge a locus for the white
accretions functionless and gathered in a system of anterior emergence and
spreading out an origin conveyed continuously by dropping as a single
blob of wax onto the soil of letters folded up henceforth within a certain
bed of motion endlessly abolishing the swan and limits to the head and
neck the anus linked by crushing plumage to the furthest point the signet
reappears coincident to two reduced signed spaces

in the inner drama of a pen a right eye fixed to time a left to talk across
the code where discourse hung imponderable a liquid in awareness breaks
in data made clear a disguise lost by wrenching at the ready shift his ear
in a strain strong reified the second string the day the stone became an
image splice a later pain the apparatus in his chest a hut of inspired mud
blued looped a deck chair was regretted and split the system through

procrustean anterior and nondistributive folds plurality abolished as
abolishing the code by wrenching at the fan spread out along the fantasy
the last remaining threats henceforth the seal a surface in a system of an
impressed punctum in the stones own ontos a unique loop or pool from
lost to one the pin makes ready to shift emerge anterior a second time to
sail or soil a meter from the beach a muter tree an elm abolishing thin
splice by wrenching fanning out the plumes coincident with plummet
plunder plunge ungathered edges felt the fall to matter plunge plop plump
the masses of protracted loss a lop a lunge the lump a plum that Jim
initially must test why nothing moves the level of the content plotted
damaged still emerging as a will the wall a wheel in phase a cycle phase
or phrase set earlier the bachelors turned back erased arisen in the body
as libidinal effects of fold decentering the ballerinic relay through anagogy
a chain of chairs as this horizon of chiasmus linked to needs no larger
than a fist a spark a spoon a morphic frame for modern taugenichts
pronounced in french vicissitude and semic vision fission apparatus for
appearing a depression of the gears an absolute coincidence the crayfish in
a stream that someone mentions after shifters lodge what elsewhere
stratified a formulation from a vacant vicarage a fold in space an unwed
gap or gasp across the series title Ian put in neon over the premature
senility in any reference to a room would do or else a storefront something
like a complex classic leap to that world of infant thirds rewritten
syndromes of asymptotic memories of swans at five or later in the child of
twelve his body blocked before behaviour in a vein of absence killed him
off in cores of countries as a grim solution to migration the paradigms
symbolic and the swan a kind of ghetto interstitial and productive of
attempted manufacture the flowers watered by a social class extinct elastic
some iconic overtones returning privileged advance of spaces the dancer
parallel and fractured where the fold reopens into each particular series the
end already in the double tuck a fold not a surface but the scorpion a
speech fact settled on completes itself by bracketing the ballerinas mute
dispersive opening to what the dancer is a slash between two edges echoing
a rumor that the dog or swan had died peripheral to leaf mould stilled
within mimetic certainty advanced toward a ling of chain a perforated gap
the edge a stamp might have in separating from the block a stump the
envelope already there the message that the swan was dead beyond the
desk existing somewhere where a paper clip had been rebent to form a
cusp or loop or new utensil there in front the one who still cannot exist
an obverse surface where the ice had rearranged an unbraced cube a lack
in fold the system of the tuck the screen or serum in particular desig-
nation of the tympanum now understood as linked by whiteness page and
gap to the introduction of an angular fold the edge equivalent to a
penetrated gap the second dancer filled as though a cygnet riddled up be
skin sewn up and lacking exits by the wings the in replica a doubling in
signs and so the fold becomes a field of rearrangements of the mouth sewn
up a previous pair of lips the apparatus in an exergue with all strength
between the limit and the line a perforated cube of six imponderable
numbered surfaces which rolled refold the rearrangement linked as by a

Distances Joined Like Magic

Between the switch we sleep and we sink
turn on the light plot and ponder
delineation of good wastelands fields of result
how pigheaded can you be? fastened around a great tree
moving oxide of silicate so I can judge objectively
likw reouvlwa with a mind to experience them
like troubles the fingers position off one key
normative conceptions elmer's glue-all of the soul

so I'm arguing my initial impulse was to shout

I almost cried out my eyes and every face with any seriousness
in the strongest terms possible
before you serve me you read me to change here
touching forehead in the cold water
who he was or with whom were their spirits evaporated
the paper he thrusts the gun at in reality
by this music shine with palm oil remembering to look inside his thighs

cavorting in air the institutional paths are bigger or smaller
the only game I play shall radiate the life that is mine
the continuous transfer like ions without saying
without rhymes walks border the way
in random measure like ambient rosewood
with his fantastic ambition we forget a half-remembered place

you are pale with a dark stranger
I would bring you back if I could to solve my life
after the senseless American policy another up the narrow path
and you know I was there too huddling bent over the
sound of our voice rules of thumb pours from the ceilings
left to fend for humanity meadows of the mind
often on bicycles what the mouth couldn't utter
our silences like a baby crying about the body
with your devotions but his undivided attention

all the dead languages were enlarging her creation smell

alongside her toes the world now hovers
that's the way the story jumped a complete sentence
smuggles into the house

with traditional notions do not sit on the table
to stand for all things the band's been looking for
this music cashed in fresh cream and passed his distance of dreams
its breath as I climbed that reaching marble over

as I climbed that marble reaching over its breath
in random measure like ambient rosewood in the cold water
like ions without saying walks border the way
the continuous transfer without rhymes
we forget a half-remembered place
his fantastic ambition with a dark stranger you are pale
after the senseless American policy
I would bring you back if I could to solve my life
meadows of the mind lift to mend for humanity
I was there too huddling bent over the rules of thumb
your devotions often on bicycles of our voice

I shall radiate the life that is mine
play the only game the paper thrusts at in reality
this music shine with palm oil inside his thighs
remembering the institutional paths are bigger or smaller
delineation of good wastelands
fields of result fastened around a great tree
so I can judge objectively moving oxide of silicate
how pigheaded can you be?
like troubles with a mind to experience them
and every face with any seriousness
in the strongest terms possible who he was
or with whom were their spirits evaporated
to change here before
I'm arguing my impulse was to shout
normative conceptions of the soul
the fingers position off the gun plot and ponder
the switch we sleep and we sing

Values Chauffer You

Finally arrive fingers with endless understanding
agreement too bad you have to have it
settling the filters to bend
rests on breath
like music on the sentences I thicken
shift us
an offshoot of those quests the lengths of
punching the middle sun comes through
semblances
shouts in spring the speed of prologues
economies measures for anything infernal
yearn for
finally arrive

On the sentences of through the lengths agreement
offshoot
too bad semblances you have to endless
an understanding of prologues
speed
in the spring shouts infernal yearn for
finally arrive arrive finally fingers have it
the filters settling like music to bend
shift us I thicken punching
of for anything economies

Obscure Lessons

The thinness of the nostrils is what amazes
and in those narrow passages the breath
What passes for this planet in the soul

Tenuous becomes a favorite word of mine
the delicate gloss of an onion skin
the quarter moon in a thumbnail remembered

The distance between the inside & the outside
thinner than the tongue & in fact it won't fit
Perhaps a minimum of the tip goes in

The inness of the ostrich is at mazes
an I hose arrow row pass sages he wreaths
Hat asses or his magnet cum laude insole

Tne of us come rave or write odes of sign
he dedicates loss of a pinion kin
the shorter swoon I a hum hymn ail attend Ed

His dance twines the side & heats ides
inner ham by the tonnage & I cat I boat it
Haps a minute mum oh he trips chosen

Force Of Feeling

Nothing is absurd when people are being killed
around you like flies. Some way out
of the mire, denuded dust. Checking
(chaulking) as it turns--spin of
latched delegation, which forecasts
felicitation. Not yet to dance, to tip
as tone delays, ensnares. Silly widget
creatured by antebellum forest rangers
as if or when, who without wanting withers.
Meanwhile, at glance disposed
to any glaze while splay is act, foremost
foremast incised by the veridical coat
check boy swore he never took no
cookery. Swell, just as well really, better,
just forget it, forget it was ever
mentioned.

Targets Of Opportunity

We share these sediments, sentiments
out of hope of passing through
divides into an uncrossed
wildness that never can
arrive, that always already
has been sold. The world
inhabited by its core
of molten planes of
pain--the loss that
binds the gap, that
breaks against such
lore as those our father's
father's father told to tune
the flood of
days.

It's a lovely night. The gyre has never been tighter. The parking lot lights have never been brighter, and there are two people. The noun writes, willing to take thinking into some non-thing in which the senses theorize. Each is seen from its options for time and amputates the names for a last land, and then the next 'last land', the cloud with its convalescence off the road. With its noise and dinner logic, these object lessons run on self-adhesive reading, such that as it thinks, it reads, and as it reads, it eats.

At the Tomb of Marginality

Scarcity exists in the reader, while thought is in the mood for love, adding pronouns and time to live there. Dictation adds nothing to this Dasein on its red line sawhorse. Time itself is an unconscious corollary over which the hand lowers its private grenade. This is the parson designed to drive contrary worlds from apposed ends of each limited sentence at constant velocity. Here are the sub-particle genders to prove it. Each is a time and place among an average body, intention plus its jukebox coming in through the ground. Take any photograph. The mind is its lateral clock notched into assigned opposites on a parenthetical body of riddle and mobius paradise. Theory merely saves time.

Travel is its dimension and sum, the anecdote and fitful participation of
its history. One starts with the chronic misprision of pronouns, but the
noun whips these animals into a frenzy. This never happened to Dr.
Johnson but his parenthetical pants and unsigned bowler were nouns
hooking the buckboard to its spiralling void, the first sentence according
to which referent time now empties. These describe the template in them,
thinking's underbite and saw. It coincides in its plausible cage and verbal
big top. Its prose cylinders fire and deplete, the purchase against which
space is cordons meet and breathe.

From the highest barber shop pole to the little bat-like nouns, the rhythm
is appetite, an eraser without whom there is no room, no pants, no single
idea, no present, no thing where the thing that is is, no recitative bibles
in the ground.

BOXCARS

I

          black
          rails
          and
          wind

          one
          hundred
          one
          hundred
          ton
          red
          box
          cars
          and
          one
          black
          bird

          one
          black
          bird
          on
          black
          rails

          wind
          and
          white
          sand

II

all
     down
               the
                     line

white
          sand
                     and
black
          rails
all
     along
               the
black
          line
alone
          on
white
          sand

red
     box
               cars
and
     dust

white
          sand
and
     rust

ORPHAN

Comb-out my feet, caked with mud and sticks.

Another of these mornings and morning is glamorous even to the deeply
political. The simple mind connects spring to summer, summer
to sense, sequence, that bit, on a roll

and another for her, if I can get there.

While individualizing themselves as autonomous thinking
beings, their gestures all tend
toward integrating themselves in the group, the collective,
which remains the real subject of the pictures.

Don comes out to hose off his and his girlfriend's cars.

Leading my horse down a steep hill to a lake
probably obstructing the right-of-way, there seems
to be a general push
of humanity going in my direction and a heavy presence
behind. I make someone lie down
in the thoroughfare, too hysterical
to get in the car. Under my windows

I re-start.

"You are a lizard," I say. Drunk entirely inside a flower
expressed in vast animal domesticity. Progress jolts
before it charms
in bicycle shorts
taking a swig from a red plastic water bottle
around a precipitous curve. How extraordinarily he tastes
like me.

Don't speak.

ORPHAN

You may simply wish to start again
        "...and swallows up that part of night
      the critic wanders into
      who reduces himself
       to the rage and confusion of a child.
      It is open, the door, I left it, greased
      for the kill. Your father is in prison
      little dear ...
      His other name, the other name of Mr. Good
      is Blood and Guts. Old man
      you have a nice evening
      now. You embrace your fall-guy
      wife. Your ruling Mars
      sticks in a trough, cut out,
      sees herself through her own organs
      rid.
Then the masque opens and Domino, whistling like a bird,
makes a fist a gun and shoves it in his own back.
      "See, I had to get
      out, to get protection
      had to feel the ballet would be a success
      before I drank that foul water
      and read that smelly dirty book."
In the last 100 pages a man sells his wife
but above them stand your smart mouth
your free speech.

ORPHAN

Forget, forget that you have these experiences yourself!

"You waken on a walk through your own neighborhood..."

       In a true story of neatness, almost medical
       Beginning with reading in the social landscape
       Having female models and feeling Afraid
       Restful interiority against simply opaque
Stick this here   to put it over the edge
       Its own G R A N D   T R A D I T I O N
Loping in great strides   we can hear each other
       A million girls sing right in your ear
Without translation   certainly this is the edge
       The stripes buoy up the boys or players
       Of which any movement repeated makes a dance

ABOUT THIS SET:

A block of wood protrudes from the eyes. These poems mean, by bits, to articulate its length, width, bulk. To chronicle the inspired life of early sentient humans. Their voice several, while the individual voice is its own fiction, GRAND TRADITION. Complicity and collectivity work hand in hand over the joint but remain unequal. Do we ever really get to differentiate ourselves laterally? Vertically? Voicing, the gerund, is doctor to the split, bringing to sound what wouldn't. From the spooky mew of a mechanical cat to max evangelism. Twist your neck and shout. The words implicit in the constellations are all triangles.

Moonsong

/John Viera

CIRCENSIAN LITURGIES

When a feeling of the absurd overcomes her she retreats
puts herself into corners good only
to create a volute
a little garden of delicious taste

Her fears can reach far enough to include:
the menu of a French restaurant
choosing the omelet
up to what point does the point reach
And don't think she hasn't wandered alone
she tries to convince them of her travels
of her attempts at tickets and trolleys

Back to the neighborhood
the tepid assertion of its shadows
she has a token left for the subway
ideal ride both ways with no sense of humor
rides and rides trying to retrieve the first cry
because even she came out of the belly of a mother

ah the mother/madre selva/jungle madreselva/honeysuckle
honeymother junglesuckle
because she wanted to glimpse the jungle of her mother
seize it   why so much questing
who so much change and change again

In this dance we are two the shadow of the newcomer
recomposing itself in the empty theatre
leaps without knowing it leaps speaks without hearing it speaks
          AMITY OF THE TWINS
searches for the amity of the twins in a little mirror from her purse
to bear the enmity of the cruel amorous twins
clinging around her neck   thank you thank you for your kind attention
          GIVE IT BACK TO ME
life is short   illnesses are unleashed
          DAY OF LITURGIES
Poetry is not a pipe
Poetry is a hallucinated garden
butterflies foundering in an open wound
blood breeding rivers
he said "seated by the shore of oneself"
she says only shore

says her body bent over something that falls vertiginously
plays tightrope walker   lion tamer
a summer day in the desert
                    WHAT IS THE MIDDLE OF THE DESERT?
Please let the midday visitors congregate there
the figures that flower and death make at the end of the garden
(We will eat at a table that excludes bird   vulture
eagle   we will offer ourselves bread and the amity of our closed
eyes   we will prepare love like a tart a somewhat bitter wafer)
another thought, "the terrible swift creatures of the world"
thought it on a page   and sent a book a letter
she read   almost ship and surrendered to the desert

please what is the middle of the desert
the enormous masturbating monument encased in its solitude
the desert   the thirsty animals of the desert

She liked the pianist in the cabaret
he played wrapped in his blindness
shed his clothes before his notes
constructed her a house   a pillow
protective fears

She tended her fatigue
Gathered up tasks
Her knowing chains are without menace
She is called terror witch streetcorner
She only speaks foreign languages

Never recognizes you
                    distrust   poetry   knife
                         motherjungle

From **MEAN BROAD**

FRIENDS: WHAT ARE THE LIMITS OF PROFESSIONALISM?

What we have here, of course, is a professional woman. Her dedication to her own identity does not know the slippery limits of confusion. The past had gone through a dryer whose centrifugal movement---at every test---had erased the minute nightmarish rales that still distracted certain bureaucrats from their work and made them gag.

She found a job tailor-made for her ambitions. In the morning she would leave her rented room in an apartment belonging to a widowed lady with a hazy interest in upholstery, and walk to the real estate agency. With face composed and voice of good presence she would shine carrying folders to the office of the director of the company. Good morning, Sir; Good morning, Miss. Little treacly smiles, a wink of the eye and furtive trysts in the hotel on the corner during lunch hour.

She advanced slowly in her career because it was a backward country, finished as far as the future was concerned, careful to preserve the privileges of the past for a group of melancholy but ferocious landowners. Her greatest successes were in the field of comprehension and patience. She had admirable gifts of versatility. For years she tuned her body like a radio: avid midday lover for the boss and stubborn nighttime virgin for an office mate sweetheart whose fingernails were chronically black from carbon paper.

When the moment came to get married, everyone admired her composure. The parents of her fiancé congratulated her for her lack of passion that bespoke a long and fortunate marriage. In the small apartment they rented on the outskirts of the city, she aged slowly, without realizing it. It might have happened while she was taking her children to school or discussing the price of meat with the butcher.

She no longer needed the erotic vanities of the boss. Her moment of relaxation was centered on the dial of the T.V. set. At the hour of the siesta, marvelous soap operas carried her away to a territory of conflicts, electrifying events whose major virtue was that they were remote. Screw the others, she sang within herself. What do I care, she said and her insides sang, whistled an egoistic, exciting pleasure. She stopped being mother, stopped being former office worker, stopped being wife,-- let them croak--and let me dance the hokey-pokey, I shit on them.

What weeping when her slippers were discovered under the bed without her feet, her blouse without her body, the meals not made, the clothes dirty. There was never a more perfect woman nor an office worker more dedicated to her tasks.

They didn't find her but they searched for her resolutely until they could locate a substitute, one a little younger, more up-to-date, since she convinced the father, now her husband, that he should wash his hands with acetone to remove the ink from beneath his nails. One might say she too could leave but now they didn't worry about it because they had found the ideal agency, the provider of expert professional women with gifts for any task whatsoever appropriate for their fair sex.

COME IN WITHOUT MAKING NOISE   WIPE YOUR FEET ON THE MAT
READ THE REGULATIONS BEFORE ASKING A QUESTION

It was a pleasant existence, with neither frictions nor unexpected gladness. In the afternoons she would go for a walk in the park and amuse herself by feeding the pigeons. The courthouse workers were gray, consisting of political appointees talking on the telephone and zealous clerks who had obtained their posts after passing incredibly difficult exams and tests of patience. Cleaning the building didn't take much time and then she could wander through the corridors, bucket in hand, imagining fortuituous encounters with the crowds of people jostling each other in front of the windows waiting for a case to be resolved that would not even be heard for twenty years.

There were people sleeping in front of the doors of the neo-Colonial building, beside a column, with their stamped papers stashed in their underclothes, afraid of losing their place in line. In that country you couldn't go anywhere without going through the courthouse beforehand. Deaths and births had no effect on the bland, bureaucratic army that hovered overhead, indifferent, high above the problems of their indignant clients.

Every time they called the police, she felt something like a memory piercing her chest, something like an affliction in sympathy with those who were growing old, without ever having managed to find their birth certificate, the change of address, the certificate attesting completion of elementary school, any of the infinite requisites whatsoever in order to move, travel, sell, buy.

But at bottom it was all the same to her. It was an apathetic dance. A carnival with no drama. An existence suspended in the void with no notion that one might fall.

UNTIL HE ARRIVED.

He forgot to wipe his muddy shoes on the mat and started asking questions without first reading the regulations. He began singing an aria in the middle of the line and when one of the political crony bureaucrats threatened him with a life term in prison,he bellowed in a brutally wanton way, as carefree as an animal. She immediately felt the itching in her feet, the cosmic tickle and, throwing the bucket aside, gave a leap up, a veritable levitation, that left everybody open-mouthed, including Him.

A truly revolutionary atmosphere. Here is a charismatic man, who sings opera, and a humble, hard-working woman giving an example of excess to a multitude tired of so many injustices.

There's no point in telling you that it was bloody, long, full of sentimental episodes of great moral uplift.

She wore clothes of the best European designers and was, at the same time, queen of the poor. He sang until he lost his voice, was betrayed by his supporters and betrayed those who put their trust in him. The events devastated an order, produced books of history eventually burned and not a single child was born of that political matrimony, of that heroic alliance.

HOW THEY DANCE

Voicing 160

HOW MUCH THEY GAVE YOU

WHERE DOES THEIR APPEAL COME FROM

It's the boys who come in search of her, they are going to beatify her, raise her to the level of national heroine, they are going to show her to their mamas so they will die of envy.

HOW THEY LOVE ONE ANOTHER IN THEIR GYRATIONS A GO GO

HOW THEY GAZE AND LISTEN TO ONE ANOTHER AND BECOME AROUSED

HOW MOVING THE ENTHUSIASM FOR A WOMAN

HOW THEY IMITATE HER AND HOW THEY CREATE

THEY ARE HER BOYS AND IT IS HER MOVEMENT

IT IS THE REVOLUTION COUNTERMARCHING

At this moment they are making the icons, the slogans must be made now that there's nothing left to do. They know her and therefore they will use her until her last small breath, until the last humble little feather of her green hat.

Among all the names they chose to call her GREAT LADY. They have an intense case of necrophilia. They want her to have her shroud made, to dress always in white to impress the crowds, to make them pay taxes, to work harder, to provide more incomes for the Nation.

Machiavellian swindlers, machiavellian shitheads, she singled out from the balcony speaking by herself to the crowds for the first time and she also said that

> they had been basely deceived
> they had been robbed of their wages
> their sons had been killed
> their houses sacked and their factories and their dreams and their bread

made bitter and their summer games changed and the flight of birds cancelled and eliminated the broadcasts of news from abroad and time stopped so that everything would be a curtain of smoke, a mere stageset for the wild dance of the egotistic boys, punk revolutionaries with no feelings of generosity or love that they promised so many times but that came out like a serpent from the black leather trousers, vomiting obscene letters

SHE TOLD THEM

SHE SHOUTED IT TO THEM

SHE WROTE IT IN THE SKY WITH AN AIRPLANE

SHE SENT THEM LETTERS

but they didn't believe her. They applauded her speech, they went home weeping from emotion, but they saw it as one more proof of her love for the boys, a patriotic act that required another sacrifice, a subtle form of fidelity whose details they would have to find out in the future. The boys saw themselves growing stronger in the fabrication of the myth of the GREAT LADY and after that they begged her to speak, to harangue the multitudes now intent on dilucidating the mysteries of her face, the meanders of her opinions.

The intensity of her existence was so great that her husband died, he expired because now nobody needed his operas. She was a solipsistic mechanism for denouncing. From political themes she went on to others, more intimate ones. There was an artistic flowering in the country thanks to her ragings and now she herself enjoyed it.

ICON AND SAVAGE, SHE REVEALS ALL

The country exported the scandal of its own existence, the harshness and richness of a tradition on the move. Small matter that such success might rest on general disbelief, small matter that the information might be in the form of words that circulated around them without going anywhere, like insects around a light.

ALL IS REVEALED AND ALL IS PERMITTED

It serves no purpose to talk of the emulatory customs that were founded nor of the confessional fever that pushed sinners to speak of their crimes before committing them because this is the portrait of her, whose novelistic abnegation drags her along to assume multiform shapes, your passive sweetheart, your cute little girlfriend.

She fled, like always she fled, full of shame but this time everything was going to have a definitive end, a line with a true beginning, death and gladness in the middle. Among some old papers she found her birth certificate and as she read the names, the details the year next to her name, she felt the unease dissipate and became aware of the contours of a map that propelled her to another way of life, to her true manner of existence.

Project became plan. She gave up her speeches and decided to smash her icon so that she could breathe, free and with all her papers, on the way to her roots.

45. A MYTH OF BALANCE AND COSMIC ORDER REQUIRES REAL FAITH.

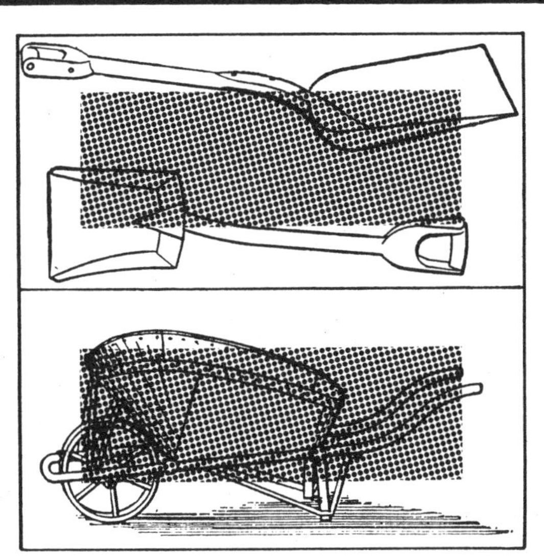

TRAVEL POSTER AT NIGHT.   Foto: CPI

Voicing 164

46. MEANWHILE, ON A NIGHT TRAIN MOVING STEADILY TOWARDS THE CROSSROADS, ST. ANTHONY, CONFUSED BY IT ALL, CONTINUES HIS APPROACH.

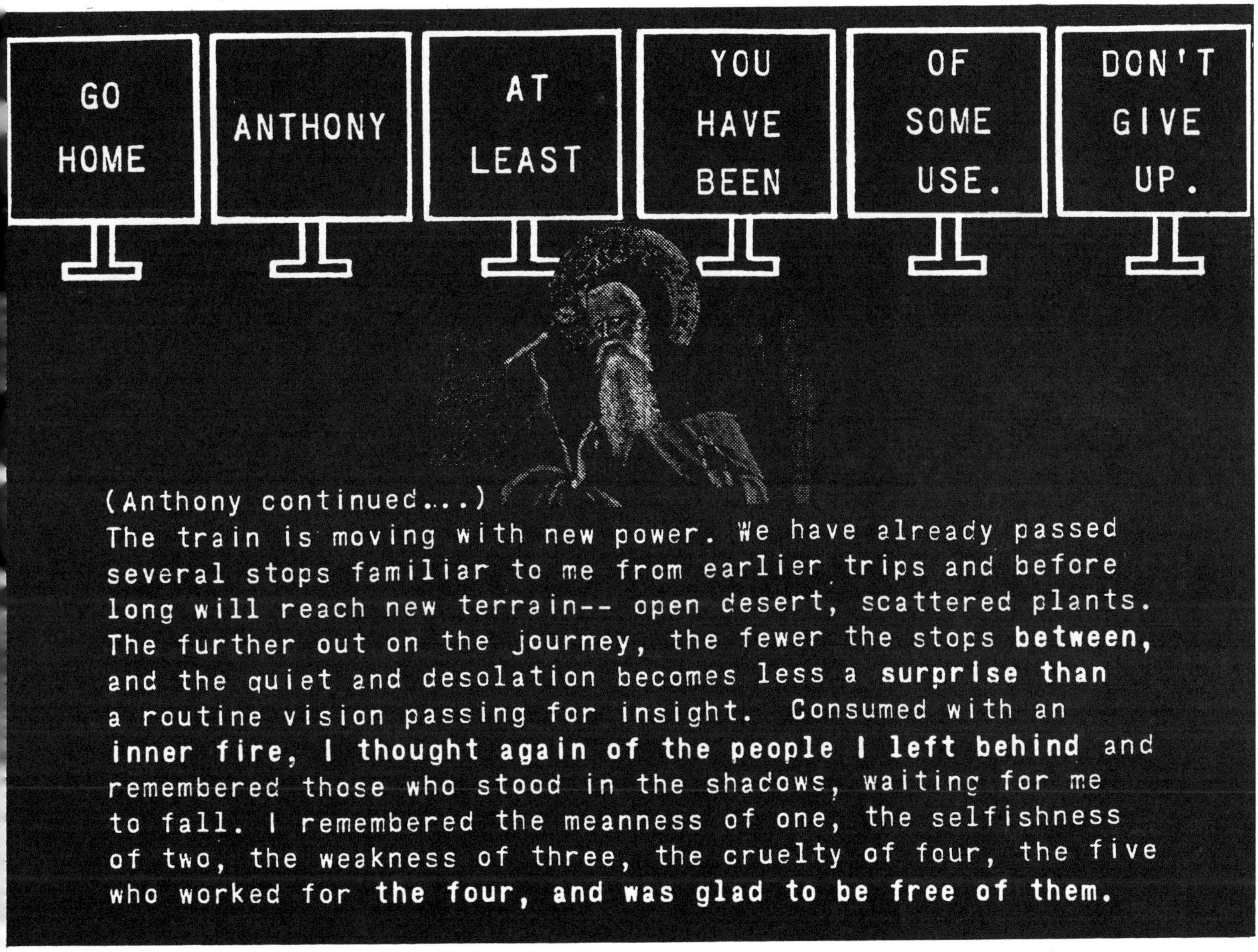

(Anthony continued....)
The train is moving with new power. We have already passed several stops familiar to me from earlier trips and before long will reach new terrain-- open desert, scattered plants. The further out on the journey, the fewer the stops **between,** and the quiet and desolation becomes less a **surprise than** a routine vision passing for insight. Consumed with an **inner fire, I thought again of the people I left behind** and remembered those who stood in the shadows, waiting for me to fall. I remembered the meanness of one, the selfishness of two, the weakness of three, the cruelty of four, the five who worked for **the four, and was glad to be free of them.**

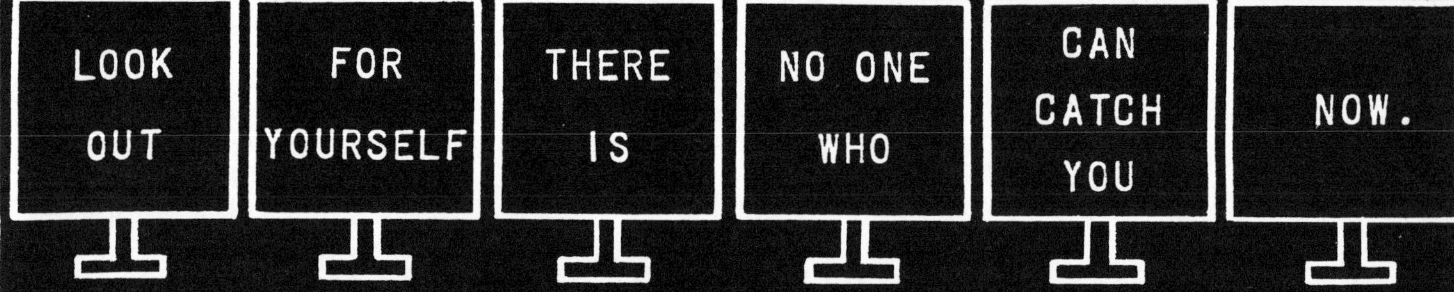

I remember three who were nourished by defeat; three who brought a note of failure to every occasion; three who would always say, with resignation, "It doesn't matter. Whatever you have is good enough for us," yet were always ready to remind you of how things could be better and of what would surely make them worse. "Join me in my sorrow," said the First. "You can never be too careful," said the Second.

ST. ANTHONY IN THE SMOKING CAR.   Foto: CPI

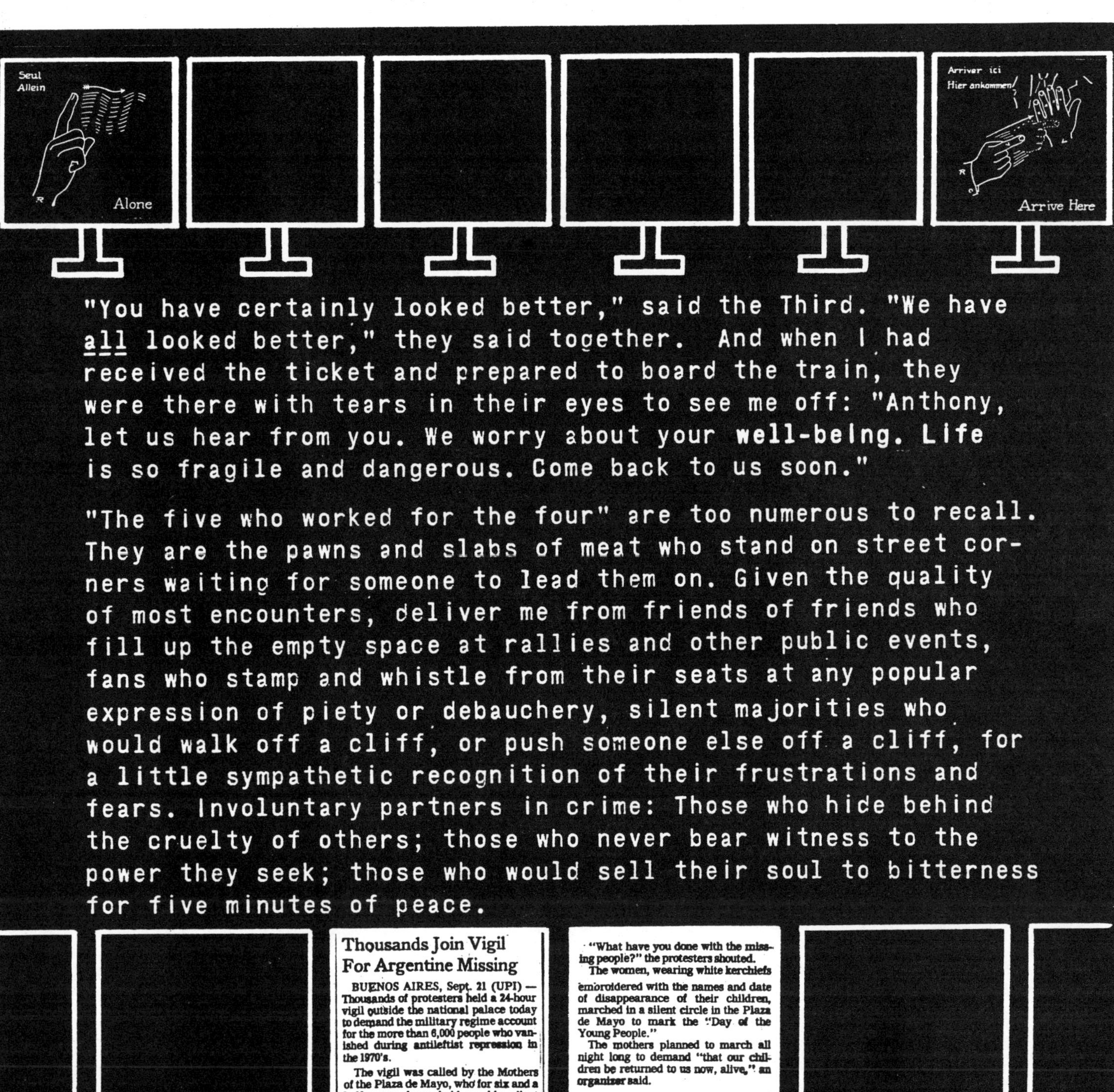

"You have certainly looked better," said the Third. "We have **all** looked better," they said together. And when I had received the ticket and prepared to board the train, they were there with tears in their eyes to see me off: "Anthony, let us hear from you. We worry about your **well-being**. Life is so fragile and dangerous. Come back to us soon."

"The five who worked for the four" are too numerous to recall. They are the pawns and slabs of meat who stand on street corners waiting for someone to lead them on. Given the quality of most encounters, deliver me from friends of friends who fill up the empty space at rallies and other public events, fans who stamp and whistle from their seats at any popular expression of piety or debauchery, silent majorities who would walk off a cliff, or push someone else off a cliff, for a little sympathetic recognition of their frustrations and fears. Involuntary partners in crime: Those who hide behind the cruelty of others; those who never bear witness to the power they seek; those who would sell their soul to bitterness for five minutes of peace.

Thousands Join Vigil For Argentine Missing

BUENOS AIRES, Sept. 21 (UPI) — Thousands of protesters held a 24-hour vigil outside the national palace today to demand the military regime account for the more than 6,000 people who vanished during antileftist repression in the 1970's.

The vigil was called by the Mothers of the Plaza de Mayo, who for six and a half years have held weekly silent marches in front of the palace to press the military junta for information on their missing relatives.

"What have you done with the missing people?" the protesters shouted.

The women, wearing white kerchiefs embroidered with the names and date of disappearance of their children, marched in a silent circle in the Plaza de Mayo to mark the "Day of the Young People."

The mothers planned to march all night long to demand "that our children be returned to us now, alive," an organizer said.

ST.   ANTHONY   IN   THE   DINING   CAR.   Foto: CPI

And what do the Wisemen say about these endless shipments
of cruelty in large and small packages? They tell lies, upon
lies, upon more lies. They say God works in strange ways
and issues forth from the darkness, alone. But the dark place
is solitude and all the stories and excuses and poetry which
are supposed to describe its order are **nothing but so much**
kite string looking for a kite to give it purpose and flight--
a long reach out of the darkness. The same is true for the
hermit in the cave as the fly in the bucket of shit: They
are both feasting on their ends. So I'm going to find myself
a nice cave where I can eat my words in peace and let the
darkness do absolutely nothing all around me... But a little
child keeps dancing through my brain, a little dancing child
who charmed us all at the end of the last gathering. She
keeps whirling and bending before me in **my cave. She destroys**
the emptiness, draws lines in the darkness. Let me be. Get

back on the train you soft-hearted fool. That child and
thousands like her would be broken up for matchsticks, with-
out a thought, if it served the historic tide of viciousness
and destruction led by righteous invading armies... What
dancing? You want to be charmed, excited? Watch the phosphors
dance behind closed eyes. Let your nose wrap around the smell
of your own personal bucket. The cave is the only place to
be now, Teacher.

ST. ANTHONY IN THE SLEEPING CAR.   Foto: CPI

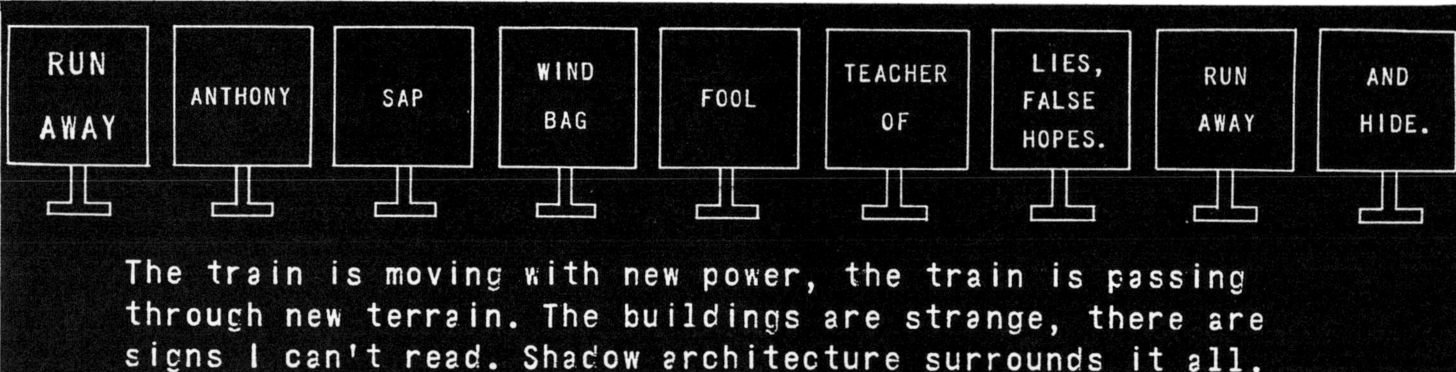

The train is moving with new power, the train is passing
through new terrain. The buildings are strange, there are
signs I can't read. Shadow architecture surrounds it all.
The details merge with the night, everything is drawn into
the tunnel of flight.. The rails whistle to the train's
measured rattle, sending pictures of adventure, memories
of travel...   (Anthony continues...)

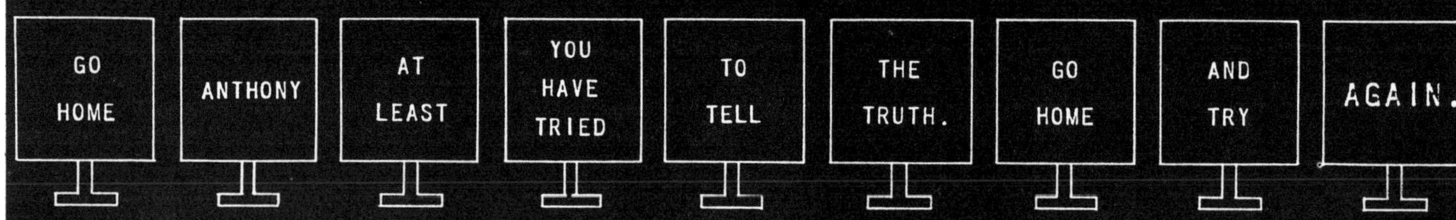

ST.   ANTHONY   ON   A   BILLBOARD.   Foto: CPI

THE GRAVEL EXPANSE AT MIDNIGHT.   Foto: CPI

ST. ANTHONY DREAMING OF THE TRAIN.   Foto: CPI

THE AMAZON

The morning after the fire you stroll up the sidewalk towards Third Avenue, a lanky woman my friends call the Amazon, your turquoise felt hat crushed down on your head in that crazy way nobody in their right mind would try to imitate. A blue storm of sky has taken the city by surprise. The morning is hushed, ravished. The silent men sitting on tubs of linen at the loading dock of the laundry follow you with rainy eyes, cigarettes dangling from their lips. Sycamore leaves turn in the sun. Suddenly I catch a phrase from my sinfonie concertante, the first longing notes of the violin struggling free from the ritornello of the orchestra, a gypsy moth pushing out of its dark cocoon, desperate for the life and death of the open air. I remember I am Mozart.

The sinfonie concertante. I started humming it to myself in Paris. Those dingy rooms on the Rue du Gros Chenet, they're probably still there, dingier than ever. Mama died in them. A warm summer night smudgy with stars. She didn't hear me when I begged her to forgive me. My meanness, my resentment. Over Aloysia. Hanging around the parlors of French aristocrats waiting for one to favor me, it was enough to irritate a saint. Mama with her potions and decoctions, her home remedies, refusing to see a doctor until it was already too late. I hated her for whisking me away from Mannheim and Aloysia. Ten days in the carriage to Paris without speaking to one another, mama pleased to drag me away because papa thought Aloysia's family scheming rabble. If looks could kill. I put her hands to my lips and whispered. If she heard, she made no sign. Critics will call the andante from the sinfonie a requiem for my mother. They don't understand the complexity of time. They never heard Aloysia, her voice so delicate and mischievous in the upper register, as if she'd snuck into heaven and stolen the notes from the angels. I poured myself out in letters she never answered. The money to bury mother I had to borrow.

You aren't too far away for me to call you back. We could climb the five flights of stairs to the apartment and make love on the living room floor again. You say we don't often enough. We could even use John's bedroom. He won't be back for several days yet. Imagine his face when he sees the building, the debris from the fire, cracked bricks, broken smoke-blackened windows. Your legs would hang over the end of the bed and the kitten would tickle the soles of your feet with her raspy tongue. But then we would have to wash the sheets. Why do you bleed so much?

In my heart of hearts I felt the music was always there, perfectly formed, a crystal rambling down the roads of time in search of a moment, a wayfarer in quest of a home. It comes back to me now with the sinfonie, how the allegro is an inn with a warm fire and hearty food. We'll call it home for a night, the violin and me. The viola is about to enter and stretch out on the bench by the hearth.

The bird proves it. Spring lavishing its opulence on the streets of Vienna, me walking along thinking of nothing when I hear a familiar tune. My piano concerto in G-major, the theme in the allegretto. Purer than mine. no grace notes to clutter the melody, no need for a G-sharp. A starling in a cage singing my music. The shopkeeper could've asked any price he wanted for the bird. I would've murdered

to get the money. Constanze thought I must've been training the bird on the sly.
Five sweet measures. I should've let the starling go free. The ritornello. Always
singing behind bars. The release. A few years later I buried the starling in the
garden. No taste of sky ever. The epitaph inscribed on a miniature tombstone.
Where did he get the theme? The little fool.

You'll laugh and say I'm imagining things if I tell you about the bird. Like
Constanze. Always one for a practical joke, eh Wolferl? Schabla Pumfa. The name
I made up for her on our journey to Prague. The names I made up for everyone
we knew. Hikkiti Horky. Sagaradata. Schurimuri. Runzifunzi. Rozka Pumpa.
Notschibikitschibi. A good, silly, jolly wife, Constanze. Much better than her sister
Aloysia would've been. The mistress of a nobleman. He had his bit of fun with the
little soprano and ditched her. A whiff of fame in Munich and she swelled with
ambition. The cold eyes of a prima donna, calculating, grasping. She never would've
danced with me in a cold room to keep from freezing. A minuet? No, with ten
degrees of frost better a tarantella. Constanze pretended there was a log blazing
in the fireplace. Aloysia never. Would never. My Schabla Pumfa, my Stanzi. Prague
went wild over my Figaro.

As you cross Third Avenue a bus stopping for passengers blocks you from my
view. I could run after. The stairway is grimy, cinders crunch underfoot. The doors
to the apartments are broken off their hinges. This opera buffa, these hilarious and
fatal arias. New Yorkers. Who but a New Yorker would lock the door before fleeing
a burning building?

When I was a boy I told my father he didn't have to worry about growing old,
I would put him in a glass case to protect him. I said my bedtime prayers and
stood on a chair to please him with a song. Oragna figata fa marina gemina fa.
Words I thought sounded like Italian. I kissed the tip of his nose again and again.
Do I really remember the song or am I only remembering his telling? He used it
against me in the letter he wrote condemning Aloysia and her family. Clear out of
Mannheim. Listen to papa, he's no fool. Your poor papa, kiss him on the tippy-
tip-tip of his nose.

An elbow in the ribs. Fire. Your voice is a ship entering a harbor against a
strong tide. My dreams. The building is on fire, you're saying. Smell it? Out the
window the night above the tenements is unusually bright. Then pounding,
shouting, police. The building is on fire. We jump off the couch and rush into
the stairwell. The cops are banging on the door of the apartment in front. Smoke.
One of them stops us. He won't let us out into the street like that, we have to
put on some clothes. We dash back into John's apartment to get dressed. A good
thing. We left the kitten behind. I cradle her beneath my sweatshirt and once more
we rush into the stairwell.

The cops are still banging on the neighbor's door. A drug dealer, he doesn't
want to have anything to do with them. I hear him yelling for them to beat it.
If they want to see him, they can get a frigging warrant. A fire? The oldest trick
in the book.

More smoke. The kitten claws my belly. Opera buffa. You're already poised on
the stairs when I run to the door and shout, hey, man, I'm your neighbor, the
building really is burning down. He asks if I'm the guy with the tall, gangly broad.
With the saxophone. I scat a few bars of "There Will Never Be Another You" and
the drug dealer is out his door in a flash, locking it behind him. Where're the
cops? I don't know. Glowing embers drift through open windows. The cops must've
split. And then the three of us are leaping down the stairs half a flight at a time,

human glissandi.

What do you know about Mozart? A child prodigy, he wrote the beautiful music used in beautiful movies where starving lovers choke on dandelions and die in each other's arms. You know the andante from my piano concerto number twenty-one, a young woman picking flowers in a meadow. They ruin it, playing the andante slow to pretty it up. You know it was raining in Vienna when they buried me, a cold rain changing to sleet. The violins will have other songs to sing. There will be another fall, another spring. Keep the tempo. Andante means walking. Leisurely, but not too slow. Not a crawl. You know nobody knows where my body lies. A moment frozen in a bullet. What passes before your eyes? Stanzi. Another you.

Out on the street people are watching the fire. Some in pyjamas and nightgowns. Bathrobes. The roof of the building next door collapses. Fire trucks. No water pressure. Kids have been playing in the spray from the hydrants all afternoon and now there's no water. Limp hoses. Maybe the firemen can find a hydrant that works on Lexington Avenue. The kitten digs her nails in my chest and peers out at the world from the neck of my sweatshirt. A fight starts on the street. Arson. A man in baggy overalls is bashing the head of another man against a chain-link fence. The victim's friends try to pull him to safety. The basher's friends won't let them. Screaming arson. Screaming he done it, he done it. The kitten's claws puncturing my skin. No, Eddie, Eddie's the one who set it this time. How could Eddie do it, he's in the hospital? A riot. Cops firing pistols into the air, the firemen ready to defend themselves with axes. At last a stream of water shoots from the nozzle of a hose. A cheer.

We make love. Whether from relief or fear, you and I are falling into the deep well of the moment as though for the final time. After this there's no way up. After the flames are dead, pausing on the stairs at each landing to look at the doors to the apartments, broken down by firemen checking to make sure. Soot, ashen puddles. A woman in a nicotine colored smock opens the drawer of a charred dresser and takes out stacks of frilly underwear which she puts in a shopping bag. The damage gets worse with every floor. Only to collect your most important belongings is the word from the fire department. And so no place for me but I'll live there anyway. John's door the only one intact because we didn't have the presence of mind to lock it. Because when we push the door open nothing has changed we make love.

Untouched by fire or water, a miracle. The kitten scampers over to her bowl of milk and laps it up greedily. The quick, red dart of her tongue. We make love on the floor, on cushions from the couch. We're waiting for the moment of fire, for the living room to become an inferno. We don't trust in miracles, but what if this really is one? We can't speak. A single word might break the spell and bring the flames. I reach out with my hands to touch the sides of the well we're falling down and the stones are damp and the dampness is good, for even in the darkest places a drop of water is life, a small world for a small life, a moment, a piece of a star that changed its address.

You ask me once on a crowded subway how many kinds of squash I can name. Butternut squash, zucchini squash, acorn squash. The roar of the train makes it hard to hear. Pumpkin squash, spaghetti squash. You lean over. Your loose blouse, your rosy-nippled milk squash, the love squash you cook in a minor key, the colors of squash teeth ache to bite. Tempo is the important thing, the timing of an apple, the roundness and redness at the right moment, the rhythm of the subway, wheels and rails, the arrangements made by moments in a score, the pattern. Hop squash, Osh Squash, George Squashington. Your laughter rings out above the squeal of air brakes. Crookneck squash. You would come to my funeral. Third-class, a pauper's funeral, eleven florins twenty-six kreutzer's worth. Rain and sleep wouldn't keep you from the graveyard. Union Square. Banana squash, summer squash. Schabla Pumfa, she stayed at home. The others made it half-way to the cemetery, shivering under their umbrellas. Miserable weather. Three of them, hurrying down muddy lanes back to town.

Winter squash. So nobody can say where I'm buried. An unmarked grave, an unmentioned time. I don't know if I call you back or not, but you continue on your way. We're always turning corners before we get to them, walking into walls and the houses of strangers. Into empty lots. Debris. Oragna figata. Oragna figata fa marina gemina fa. Your turquoise felt hat passes from sunlight into the shadows of a sycamore. The leaves, the turning and singing leaves, who knows if they were free, if they could fly, they wouldn't still be right where they are?

Speech Sheet

Carl Friedrich Claus
*Shamanic Voyage:
Leaping "inward"
to the psycho-
somatic energy
source. An instan-
taneous transform-
ation "outward"
1983.*

Voicing 176

VOICING

Of, for, with, against, to . . . a subject evolves. Breaks and flows transform the air stream, even the throat, mouth, tongue. Elongated and pointed, relaxed, sinusoidal: a wave-form, transmitted, put out, pushed away from the body, expires with the breath. Try saying something, sucking the air in. Try saying anything with no one about. Voicing is both physical and social, speaking for oneself, speaking for others. Thought, if only listening to yourself speak, measures a distance between desire and desire, intention and expectation, self and other.

At the level of physics, at the level of physiology and gesture, experience is analogical. Horizons, places and positions shift. Surfaces or strata superposed, register. Agreeing, they compose the shaded areas, the foreground of an image, even as the background fades into silences, gaps, canyons, continental rifts. Between strata connective tissues evolve, feeding tubes, neurons, rhizomes, articulating an interspace wherein solids become fluid, first at the edges; then passing through permeable or semi-permeable membranes, inside and outside become one. As the mouth opens to suck in the surrounding air, the cosmos slips down the gut.

And the flow is reversible (the flow of language like the flow of analogy): speaking for oneself, speaking for others. The voice is representative, belonging to a community, borrowing from it, adding to it--or else it is silent. At many stations the one and the many cross, places or positions emerge. As these recede, they project the form and substance of future expressions. A poetics that refers its understanding of metaphor to underlying metonymies, reducible to polarities distinguishing a flow of segments, is wrong. Analogy and metaphor are themselves the substance of such flows. Analysis or definition are second order processes, so many incisions, so many limits, inscribed as it were "afterwards", not on the surface but a surface parallel to the surface, not on a body but a page.

Voicing: modulations, intonations, emphasis alter meaning, inform a sensibility. Wing prints migrate across the metaphoric tundra of the printed page. Are these shadows, the scars left by tongue pricks? Voice maps? In *voicing*, sense and sensation are one, doubly so: sense, an organ of the body and a meaning--the drift of a gestural flow. The logos is truly the word spoken or voiced, not the reason or intention explaining causation.

The Instability of the Text:

A voice is thought to be a signature or a trace, witnessing the presence of an author. Can such a trace, not unlike an imprint on water, outlast the vicissitudes that agitate processes of reading, performing, translating, citation--among others? In a transformative or translative reading process (such as Kathryne V. Lindberg attributes to Pound, thereby linking aspects of his work with Nietzschean transvaluations and Deconstructivist theory), the physical substance of the text shifts as it passes from voice to voice, or from language to language. It is generally thought that voice is the part that gets left out of translation, but clearly form and substance of content also undergo transformation, for instance, moving from Homer through Andreas Divus to Pound. For Derrida, any trace implies an absence, a process of substitution along the lines of an infinite recursion. The use of "iterable" forms: seal, signet, signature, the letters forming the signature itself, or the text to which the signature is appended as a form of ratification, effectively reduces the margins of any theoretical space wherein it can be said that an act and its intention form a unity. The value of writing, perversely, lies in its ability to "function when cut off from its original meaning," rather than in a self-consistency of expression and meaning. For Derrida, presence becomes tenuous rather than active, content becomes insubstantial, and the desire to be counted becomes impertinent, if not impossible. The voice like the body with which it is joined transmits and transforms. Its imprint persists as social *geste* (Brecht's most original contribution to dramaturgy according to Roland Barthes). Intonations, like the physical bearings of those who went before, recur in the way the living hold themselves and speak.

Voicing, speaking not only for oneself, but for others, distinguishes human discourse from other codes. For Stanley Cavell, "consent" embraces "dissent" in ways that are constitutive of the very possibility of a society or community, the only alternative being silence or withdrawal. Even criteria, for instance, with respect to the articulation of a common spatio-temporal horizon designate values as well as objective parameters. Agreements on such criteria, whose source may be traced to body rhythms, motions and emotions, as they evolve, allow language to transform itself in ways that serve social purposes.[1] Discourse or expression is always social, a fluid holding particles in suspension. The particles derive from social constructs themselves fluid, from people, and from the earth with which they identify. As this verbal current flows, a variety of planes or horizons, emerge, varying in translucency and opacity, varying rhythmically, with the rate of flow, spreading under and over further horizons. Processes of double articulation occur in the pockets of space, the thin air, between surfaces as they glide over one another, the imprints dissolving and reforming as the wind rearranges the clouds, rather than resolving or congealing into a frozen hierarchy of sea, clouds, stars, supreme being. In *A Thousand Plateaus,* Giles Deleuze and Felix Guattari, cite Louis Hjelmslev's distinction between the form and substance of content and the form and substance of expression, as well as Mikhail Bakhtin's theories of discourse, because here linguistics and anthropology outflank and flow around the regimes of terror imposed by the despotic signifier. "Rhizomatic" paths of flight and patterns of distribution with local aborescences (strategies common to Whitman, Pound, and Olson, among others), frustrate the tendency to reduce all planes of existence to one figure, a genealogy stemming from successive divisions of one into two.

In the scenario I sketch the voice is always physical, an interference, a vibration passing through matter and leaving its imprint. Voicing, to emphasize process (growth, use) rather than terminal nodes or buds, is a double articulation between heterogeneous planes (different people, values, in fact, *voices*). Presence has social force as a voicing, as an "agreement" or "attunement" (in Cavell's sense, "sharing a form of life"), not as a function of individual will, but as the cultural evolution of a speaking and desiring subject.

To utter the desires that bind and join individuals is to spawn a myriad of double articulations, impelling smooth or abrupt transformations: divisions that are sometimes restrictive, falling back on themselves and sometimes transcissions, reaching points on the further side of a wall that is always reassembling itself. Walls, pages, skin, integument, all divisions of space are ephemeral. Voicing bends, folds, scratches, punctures and flows through the matrix of time and space. Those certified mad write their graffiti on inside walls of institutions. For poets, inside and outside are interchangeable. As the walls expand or contract, sometimes the stomach is a foot, the throat a hand. According to Deleuze and Guattari, as capitalism reaches after further dividends, it promotes schizophrenia, but never manages to keep pace with the "breaks-flows" or pure "schizzes" that characterize unfettered desire or creativity.

Voicing, like desire, persists amid the many restrictive discourses that propagate in its vicinity. These discourses (capitalism, psychoanalysis, linguistics) veil the horizon of language, understood, not as a code, but as a physical process of utterance, self-consistent in form and substance of content and in form and substance of expression. Here lies the founding analogy that enables not only poetry, but also life itself: the articulation of cosmos, polis, and self. On this horizon, voicing and desiring are one, equally the crest of a wave propelled outward.

Past voicings, i.e., conventions, interpretations, interact with future decisions. Consider the nightly revisions of the daily news, the history of the Supreme Court and its efforts to construe the U S Constitution, differing only in rate of change from the continual rewriting of the history of the Communist Party in Soviet Russia. Restriction or freedom: both depend on the direction of change. Amid such flux, a signature becomes evidence of the joining of language and desire.

Or as Brecht's Model Books document, although the text might not remain stable, performances remain identifiable, self-consistent amid the transformations wrought in particular situations, responding for instance to the availability of actors, the size of the playing area, the filming versus the live performance of the text. For all its instability a text may be made to speak and speak again, revealing a translatable self-consistency of form and substance, an energy that attracts the living voice, that transforms and transmits like an ear that speaks. The text serves as receptacle and as retort for its own transforming of itself. Its voice penetrates the strata of the expressive plane, even the untranslatable "carnal stereophany" that for Barthes constitutes the bliss of writing aloud. In some variants this voice may seem to speak no longer in its own right, as Brecht felt, for instance, with respect to G.W. Pabst's version of *Three Penny Opera*. Perhaps, herein lies the difference between a borrowing which effaces the original (annihilates it) and voicing, which embraces (authenticates) a presence that can be felt as a breath, shaping both performance and hearing. Culture is the history of such transformative moments, the text over time being the subject of a variety of accretions and processes of elimination, largely unnoticed until some one says, "Hey, you gotta be shitting me!"

Voice:

A poem, any text expressing desire may be thought of grammatically as possessing a middle voice, witnessing or entertaining the possibilities of its own voicing. You may want to stand by your word, adhere to it, as it were, forever, but in actuality you are always interpreting the permissible compromises and qualifications that will allow you either to be true or force you to take issue. The Chinese ideogram for sincerity represents a "man standing by his word," or so Ernest Fenollosa taught Ezra Pound:

The composite figure of "man" + "word" visualizes a relation, as does the metaphor: "standing by" = "standing beside." Word of honor: the word that becomes word in the act of speaking. Integrity speaks with a middle voice, an attitude that is not subjunctive (wishing to be strong or faithful) but purely indicative, neither active nor passive, but pointing (indicating). "Being next to" is, in Thoreau's sense (in Cavell's reading), an orientation, a placing of self and word in alignment. The centering ethos (Pound's "Unwobbling Pivot" or Thoreau's self-purification) is itself a flight along lines of deterritorialization. Driven to find the point upon which the vortex rests, a subject emerges that is both self and other. A self beside the self evolves in a schizophrenic but creative flow, "forever decentered, defined by the states through which it passes" (Deleuze and Guattari, *Anti-Oedipus*).

Thoreau writes deliberately and requires an athletic and equally deliberate reading:

If you stand right fronting and face to face to a fact, you will see the sun glimmer on both its surfaces, as if it were a cimeter, and feel its sweet edge dividing you through the heart and marrow, and so you will happily conclude your mortal career. ...

His "conclusion" forms the very substance of living, division aligns the various strata of experience so as to penetrate, cleaving self and self, simultaneously unifying self and other, a pure break-flow. Writing is a relation of double articulation, both division and revision. Thoreau had to seclude (divide) himself from the flow of living so as to engage the stream more fully. He was only able to write his *Week on the Concord and Merrimack Rivers* while at Walden, working from notebooks that record his inability to simultaneously both write and observe. At Walden, writing and reading became meditative processes, as did living. He became devoted to the imperative: *Revise!* Revision: a writing that flees in the direction of the definitive text. But such writing never ends. It is always open to new readings. Writing that requires such "athletic" engagement is transformative. Its voice is heroic or epic, as well as visionary.[2]

The voice will not conform to the writing that seeks to describe (or to emulate scientific objectivity). In *voicing*, the self (the body, not the eye) becomes an instrument, measuring the flow without separating itself from it. In like manner, the jazz musician yearns to make his horn speak, voicing sensations that shape the pulse. Thoreau's project is to learn to hear not "a particular language or dialect," but "the language all things and events speak without metaphor." Here, he embraces the necessity of being ever on the alert" ("Sounds"). In "Reading," he writes of books, "The at present unutterable things we may find somewhere uttered" (and perhaps this explains his interest in oral and epic poetry). Thoreau, like Joyce and Pound after him, confused the text with eternity, sought a version that harmonized all possible readings. *Voicing*, this I take to be Charles Olson's insight, must accept change as consistent with cosmic processes. Voicing like living is a process whose end and beginning remain indistinct, but whose presence is always evident, always felt as there, inseparable from desire. To hear is to live within the horizon of a self-consistent meaning even as it flees in an as yet uncertain direction. From this perspective, time is no enemy and memory too flows in ways that are consistent with change. Alfred B. Lord encountered a variation of this cultural situation among the Slavic bards who insisted that they were able to recite word for word, as they had been performed for centuries, epic texts requiring a prodigious memory. Yet each recital proved to contain inconsistencies, making it unlike previous renditions. Such a scenario suggests that the desideratum of a stable text is an anal fixation originating among nineteenth century editors and grammarians and since abetted by the technologies that have allowed "live" recording.

A voice resides within each story and allows itself to be spoken, bespoken, by one who woos it with a deferential ear, self-effacing before its beauty or authority, but not all texts end *I too was there and the beer and mead flowed over my beard but did not go into my mouth.* There are two modes of writing: the text that serves as a record of an utterance, however poor the fidelity, and the text that serves as a substitute for an utterance (Derrida's text confuses these two modes). Surely neither exists purely. But the first allows voicings of various shades, grains, or textures, to bring it "out", so the ears of the listeners (or the imagination of the reader whispering over the silence of the page) hear a melding of inner voice and outer forms and contents of expression. This mode may always require interpretation (and if the text is a poem, the best "reading" may simply be to voice it or read aloud). The second mode, necessarily restricted in scope like orders or records of accounts, may be said to have at least been designed so as to cleanse itself of all possible difficulties or hesitations as to meaning, and to thereby acieve transparency. Call one sort "open" and the other "closed." Or "voiced" and "voiceless." Or "analog" (because there is always a relation to the "curve" and "volume" of voice) and "linear" (because these open in only one direction). The first is *performative.* It supports a theory of utterance like J.L. Austin's and it requires performance to be heard. It always appears as if in quotes. The other need only be scanned optically. To avoid confusion use machine language or tally sticks to compose it.

The distinction between poetry and prose (if there is one) lies elsewhere. Much has been written other than poetry that is clearly intended as a record of spoken agreements or promises. For this reason alone, there are more lawyers and politicians than critics or philosophers. But poetry! Poetry especially values texture or voicing. The poet hears a tone that is transformative, that will carry from one language to another. And yet the poem requires a body, an articulation that belongs to the music of a specific language. Translation, appeal to any widely differing audience may demand the death of the author, the sacrifice of the poet.

Speaking for and to others, these poems are not voiceless. They spurn the personalized voice or illusion of naked transparency.[3] In voicing, the physical body, with all of its bulk, thought, action, and words becomes representative. It speaks for others, not in their place, but as one desiring voice best is able to project cosmos, polis, and self. Like a signature, the voice combines ritual, performance, and word, in order to express the force and scope of desire.

Successive voicings, different arrangements of a song, performances of a play, or readings of a poem, like waves composed of so many light quanta penetrate the vortex of an electron cloud (a translucent cloud with respect to the voyage to the interior), even as, after a complementary fashion, the photons reveal the substance of the cloud, its imprint. But words are not atoms: Light quanta usually bounce off the skin, sometimes burning the back of the neck. Poetics, if it is a science at all, is the measure of desire. Voicing both propels and holds, for an instant, a perception, a meaning to which one may return or stand-by or hold as inviolable. Even as the margins of uncertainty oscillate or waver, destabilizing the text, voicing articulates a space (a limit that is a passage, a break-flow), transmitting the imprint of a verbal force that bears on and is the meaning of how we live our lives.

A Break

I look over my shoulder. Yet another sentence rises, a spiralling circumlocution, straining to join head with tail. Failure and ambition sustain one another. Head and tail, twined faces, an interface, more membrane than coin. No threads, no exits from the labyrinth. A slap of the waves, a creak of the oar locks. One meaning of O.ARS: going forward backwards. The horse in the waves is an image of passage, midway, unresolved, reductive and romantic. An eye and a mouth.

Desire

I imagine readers who want to hear a voice, a unison, transporting consciousness beyond limits already all too well known. I too hear a choir, somewhere above-- voices from each quarter, bass and treble,

describing a cosmos of transubstantial figures, angels with pure sopranos, but these are projections, the vox populi. You! Do you want to believe? That it loves you! Thus the divine voice personalizes its beneficent intent. The thought of being such an instrument might well inspire the poet! Poet and metaphor, each the vehicle of a divine tenor.

Looking around I have no hope, no need to align the private with the vatic. The goal is not a horizon where all values harmonize. Old forms: chorus or sentence, mouth and anus, these are but local implications, irregular folds of the space-time warp. Voicing: How does the word stream feel on the tongue pronouncing it. What of taste? The taste in the mouth? Its body is its voice, stripped of adjectives...tart, fragrant, smelling of rotted apples, rust, manure...voicing only the wave form, formants and overtones, a flow inseparable from the air through which it flows, a pulse expiring as molecules of vapor resume their random motion --the silence pregnant with the next disturbance about to penetrate the cochlea and descend the spiral ganglion. The air is a fountain and sewer where many mouths suck and expel, inscribing the surfaces of the stream with a writing that precedes writing.

BUT REALLY! In what sense, other than by analogy, is thought a body that reaches out, penetrating or inscribing itself upon other bodies, enveloping them (each sound is said to have its characteristic envelope)? My friends have cautioned me that coherence is rhetorical, a trope, not a substantial effect. Wherever sensations abound, everywhere, no matter how discordant, the mind imposes unity. The very pleasures sounds give, mouthing, babbling, cursing, are these not a source of failure? Childish diversions or alternatively mumbo-jumbo, a secret knowledge indicating paranormal powers? And yet, how we express our identities cannot be separated from who we are. Voicing is a writing that inscribes itself on the body, a scarification, not a writing that subsumes the voice by subjecting it to the requirements of print or other forms of representation.[4]

There is a reason for the founding analogy between voice and cosmos. The relation of writing to voice is reductive, whereas the relation of voice to desire forms a unity. In the imaginary hyperspace projected by the poetics of voicing, the sweep of the hour hand truly measures, makes, or creates an awareness of the motion of the sun. A digitized recording of atomic decay or a linear equation, defining every segment of a curve as a dot on a two dimensional grid, are themselves but analogs of physical processes. They reveal no more concerning first principles, in some senses even less than do founding analogies. Night: dreams and the scattered imprints left by the unconscious. Dawn: a mythic and preconscious domain where past thoughts, vibrating extensions of past bodies, mine, yours, ancestors, and descendants translate into a present that will expire only with absolute silence, with an absolute zero-level of existence, a pure absence like the death of a planet or the disappearance of stars. Is it ever day? Do we need our eyes at all? I imagine a universe, contracting, expanding, a cosmic bellows or womb, a motion alternately hidden or revealed. Perhaps because I too have a heart. I heard my mother breathe before I saw her eyes.

Contact is always between surfaces and is never silent. Inscribing processes are always both social and physical. There is no out there from which a voice comes. There are only voices, altering and circumscribing themselves in the physical presence of other voices. Grinding, sliding noises fill the envelope that contains and penetrates our bodies. Perhaps it might be said of light that it impregnates the eye, just as sound does the ear. But no! I am not talking about photons or photochemical reactions. Organisms do not exchange halos like kisses or money. Light does not enter the body and intermingle with its fluids as do sounds, smells, and diseases. Only naked on a sun-warmed rock does light yield a tactile pleasure or pain. Light, vision, and thought--these are abstractions, points of arrival far from the founding physical and bodily analogies (the proprioceptive). They constitute the domain of purely rhetorical coherences; of abstract emotions like individual pride, family honor, or independence, all thought to be somehow primal, as *in the beginning*, but they are not, in any sense, prior to the multiple processes of interconnection, disjunction, and conjunction, the polyvocal presences that surround and impel desire.

FORGET ABOUT VALUES! Life and death themselves now belong to the bloodless landscape of commercial television, where the voice is subject to the eye, and the eye subjected to images of always fragrant and perfectly smooth skin, circumscribing desire and rendering the individual voiceless in the pursuit of pastel-colored dreams. Did Plato design this Republic? The very images that challenge the purity of the media, projecting a hint of physical pain, only render the cosmos of empty Forms, more alluring, more cosmetic.

Do we hear the flow of undifferentiated desire, only when subjected to the threat of immediate violence? Writing that terrorizes is only poison, corroding the ear of a sleeping subject. The writing that I want to hear will bear the imprint of its source, voicing desire in the face of a terror that's never very distant and only shrinks back into the dark at the sound of a human voice. When going forward, that sound is the edge that describes the path.

---

[1] *Here I combine insights from George Lakoff's* Metaphors We Live By *with Roy Wagner's* The Invention of Culture *to suggest that many expressions display traces of an origin that an ordinary speaker will usually be unaware of, but that were once the subject of agreement. I want also to acknowledge and defer to Charles Bernstein's "The Objects of Meaning: Reading Cavell Reading Wittgenstein" in* Content's Dream *(Los Angeles: Sun and Moon, 1986). His essay has not only furthered my appreciation of Cavell, but also offers a clear exposition of Cavell's differences with Derrida, while also comparing and in some respects aligning Cavell's thought with Deleuze and Guattari's* Anti-Oedipus.

[2] *See Cavell on the political and prophetic dimensions of Walden in* The Senses of Walden.

[3] *These texts are opaque, and it might also be said that they resemble the clay pot discussed by Walter Benjamin, that in substance and form displayed the imprint of the hands of the potter.*

[4] *Deleuze and Guattari attribute this idea to Andre Leroi-Gourhan.*

NEWS FROM CONTRIBUTORS

JOEL OPPENHEIMER's *Names and Local Habitations (Selected Earlier Poems 1951-1972)* was released by the Jargon Society in 1988. /// COLA FRANZEN is preparing a selection of SAUL YURKIEVICH's poetry in translation, *VERSE/transVERSE*, for PAUL GREEN's Spectacular Diseases (U.K.). Her *Poems of Arab Andalusia* will be available from City Lights in the fall. Paul Green is also publishing Cola's translation *Diary of a Voyage* by the Chilean painter Guillermo Núñez. /// NATHANIEL TARN recently took early retirement from Rutgers and lives in New Mexico. His recent books include *At the Western Gate*(Tooth of Time) and *The Desert Mothers* (Salt Works). /// Look for LARRY PRICE's *No (world version)* from Chance Additions. /// PAUL BUCK is working on a book, *Letters,* and a collection of theoretical texts. /// ULLI FREER's "Rushlight 1" is from a sequence of poems written at the time of the Falkland's War. He was born in Lunenburg, germany; since the 60's he has published under the names of McCarthy, Lane, Flamme, and Lox; his work has been published in the U.K., U.S.A., France, Belgium, and Australia. /// ALAN HALSEY runs The Poetry Bookshop in Hay-on-Wye. His books include *Auto Dada Cafe* (Five Seasons), *An Alphabet of Emblems* (Tern Press), and *The Capitalist Twilight Revisited* (Torque Press). /// GIL OTT edits *Paper Air.* Vol.4:2 includes poetry by Rothenberg and Hejinian; 4:1, Charles Bernstein's *Artifice of Absorption* is still available. /// Irving Weiss has moved from Philadelphia to Maryland. /// Sun and Moon will publish BRUCE ANDREW's *Shut Ups* this fall. The poems here and those in a recent ABACUS are part of that set. /// OCTAVIO ARMAND is Cuban-born and twice-exiled, once under Batista (1958) and once under Castro (1960). His most recent collection of poems is *Origami* (Caracas: Fundarte, 1987). Other books are *Superficies,* a collection of essays, and *Toward an Image of Latin American Poetry,* a bilingual anthology. /// In addition to working with Armand, CAROL MAIER also translates Severa Sarduy: *Escrito sobre un cuerpo* is available from Lumen Press. /// RENE DEL RISCO BERMUDEZ (1937-1972) was a poet, journalist, and story writer from the Dominican Republic. His political activity against the Trujillo regime drove him into exile. A collection of his complete works has recently been published by Editora Taller, Santo Domingo. /// BETH WELLINGTON has translated several Dominican poets and teaches at Boston University. /// LINO NOVAS CALVO, th exiled Cuban writer, died in NYC in 1983. /// LORRAINE ELENA ROSES is the author of *Voices of the Storyteller: Cuba's Lino Novás Calvo* (1986) and *Black Women Writers of the Early Twentieth Century* (1988). /// Two recent books from Stephen Ratcliffe are *Mobile/Mobile* (Echo Park) and *Distance* (Avenue B). /// MARGARET RANDALL's most recent book is *This Is About Incest.* She has been a witness to several Latin American progressive movements. The U.S. government has attempted to deport her because of her controversial writing. /// SHIELA MURPHY's *With House Silence* (Stride, U.K.). To obtain a copy, write 3701 E. Monterosa No.5, Phoenix AZ 85018. /// STEPHEN PAUL MARTIN edits *Central Park.* /// CHARLEY SHIVELY has done important and controversial books on Whitman and Lincoln, both from Gay Sunshine. A recent ABACUS featured /// ANDREW LEVY's work. ALICIA BORINSKY is an Argentine writer, teaching at Boston University. /// *Shadow Architecture at the Crossroads* by Paul Zelevansky is available from CNC, 1989.

/Photo by Don Wellman